HOME COOKED

recipes from the farm

PHOTOGRAPHY BY ANDREW MONTGOMERY

Gaia

For My Friends

CONTENTS

INTRODUCTION

I'm going to start with a confession – perhaps not a wise one, given that this is a cookbook of sorts. I'm not A Cook. By which I mean I'm not trained, nor in any way am I a food professional. I don't have lots of kit and I don't have the patience or inclination to spend hours fiddling about with ingredients to create foams, or smears, or gels, or whatever the latest fad is. But I do like cooking – albeit in what someone once described (not unkindly!) as a rather slap-dash way. To my mind, cooking manages to be both calming and creative. At the end of a long, tiring day, pottering about making something simple – but, hopefully, satisfying – feels like a small but significant achievement.

The recipes in this book are the ones I cook all the time. Some I've made up myself. Others I learned from my mum or from my husband Ludo. Many come from friends, others from newspaper cuttings or books. Essentially, what you are getting are recipes inspired by the various scrappy bits of paper I have tucked in notebooks, pinned to boards or shoved into a (very disorganized) file, made prettier and less disorganized.

What you will find is that I have been unashamed of not including recipes with ingredients I don't like. Like olives and butter beans. I don't have a hugely sweet tooth, nor am I someone who bakes very often, so don't expect recipes for elaborate puddings or cakes – although there are a few simple ones. In fact, all the recipes are simple, because that is what I am happiest and most comfortable cooking. And I'm extremely lucky living where I do. I may be too far away from takeaways and too off the beaten track for delivery services, but living on a small farm means I have access to fresh eggs, free-range meat from native breeds, and I can grow a certain amount of veg. I'm not remotely self-sufficient, but I can make a meaningful contribution to the ingredients I use throughout the year. And I am surrounded by wonderful local producers and artisans, some of whom you will meet in this book.

I've had much-needed help putting the recipes together from my friend Penny Johnstone. Anyone who lives within a 30-mile radius of here knows Penny. She is a professional cook who has catered for weddings, birthday parties, funerals and significant family events for her ever-increasing fan base for over 40 years. For the last few years she has prepared all the food for the people attending courses at our farm, and the food is almost always mentioned as one of the highlights of the day. Penny can make very elaborate and fancy food but, like me, what she really enjoys eating – and cooking – are good, simple ingredients that don't need mucking about with.

I cook on an Esse range cooker. I came across them thanks to Hugh Fearnley-Whittingstall, which sounds like a terrible, telly-luvvie thing to say, but we actually met when I was at River Cottage doing a 'how to keep chickens' course, soon after I moved to Wales. We were looking for a cooker at the time, because the previous owners of our house had taken their Aga with them and left a significant hole that needed filling with something. We don't have a gas supply here, so could only get an oil or electric range cooker, and I wanted something that didn't have to stay on all the time because, lovely as a warm kitchen is, it doesn't need to be warm all year round, all the time. Esses are made in Barnoldswick in a factory that has been going for 150 years. It is a fascinating place to visit and has a great café – I've filched a couple of their recipes too! But the reason I mention this is that I'm not cooking on a professional stove, or in a professional kitchen. Just my kitchen that I use every day. So this really is home cooking, inspired by the seasons; local, unfussy and easy. Happy cooking. And eating!

Notes on ingredients

Fruit and vegetables:
Not everyone is able to grow their own, so try a farmers market or veg box scheme for locally grown produce that is in season.

Eggs and poultry:
All eggs are medium, unless stated otherwise. Choose free-range or organic eggs and poultry if you can.

Butter:
Unless the recipe specifically calls for unsalted, all butter is salted – including for baking.

Salt:
I use flaked sea salt. Halen Môn is a lovely sea salt from Anglesey, or Maldon is also good and more widely available.

Citrus fruit:
Lemons and other citrus fruit used for zesting should be unwaxed. If you only have waxed lemons, just pop them in hot water for a minute and give them a rub with a cloth to remove the waxy coating.

Beef and lamb:
When it comes to red meat, grass-fed beef and lamb are the most sustainable options.

Fish and seafood:
Look for the blue label of the Marine Stewardship Council to make sure your fish and seafood come from a sustainable source, if possible. Smoked fish (such as haddock) should be undyed.

Oven temperatures:
The recipes in this book were tested in a fan-assisted oven.
If you are using a conventional oven, increase the temperature by 20°C.

SPRING

Of all the seasons, spring is probably the most eagerly anticipated. It is thoughts of renewal – of fresh green leaves, wild flowers, nesting birds – or simply the fact that the mornings are not so dark, that get many of us through the long days of winter. On the farm it is a time of new life – the exhausting pleasures of lambing time, the spring grass coming through, turning khaki-coloured fields vibrant once more. And as the ground dries, the cattle can leave the sheds and return to the pasture. If you don't think cows can skip, then watch them going out for the first time after the winter. It is joyous! The pigs too. They waddle with surprising speed – hippo-like – out into their paddocks and almost immediately dig their snouts into the grass and tear up great clods of mud until they have a lovely, mucky patch in which they can lie down and soak up the spring sun.

But spring is a capricious season. We've had years when we've been lambing in March wearing shorts and t-shirts, only to have to dig out our thermals again in April. So the food I cook at this time of year will vary – sometimes it still needs to be warming and comforting, but on days of sunshine, when the new lambs are skipping in the fields and the woods are full of birdsong, I'll make something lighter. Something that, if the mood takes me, could be taken on its plate or in its bowl and eaten outside. Colour is important too. I like my food to be colourful, whatever the season – but this time of year is, for me, a celebration of all things green.

A Soda Bread for Spring
with Parsley & Chives

I have, over the years, attempted to bake bread many times. I've created more inedible loaves and killed more sourdough starters than I care to think about. I have even had lessons – from my ever-patient and fabulous bread-making friend Jennifer of Dough & Daughters – but have finally conceded that, along with climbing Everest, making intricate, artisan loaves of bread is beyond me.

But soda bread is different. Soda bread is easy. I'd like to say even foolproof, and I'm well qualified to make that claim. And it's super-quick – no yeast, no waiting for it to prove, no kneading. Just mix everything up in a bowl, put it in a tin or on a baking tray and cook. Less than an hour later you will have beautiful, warm, homemade bread, filling your kitchen with that wonderful smell. Honestly, it is a revelation. Try it. Makes you feel like a culinary genius…

250g (9oz) plain flour, plus extra
    for dusting
250g (9oz) wholemeal flour
1 teaspoon bicarbonate of soda
½ teaspoon salt
a bunch of parsley

a bunch of chives
300ml (½ pint) buttermilk, or
    150ml (¼ pint) milk mixed with
    150ml (¼ pint) natural yogurt
oil for greasing

Makes 1 loaf
Preheat the oven to 200°C (400°F), Gas Mark 6. Mix the flours, bicarb and salt in a bowl. Chop up the parsley and chives finely and add to the flour mix. Stir in the buttermilk or milk/yogurt mixture until you have a soft dough. Tip it onto a floured work surface and knead it very lightly and briefly, just to make sure it is well mixed.

Shape into a round loaf and put on a greased baking tray or in a loose-bottomed cake tin. Cut a deep cross in the top with a sharp knife (which, according to my friend Jennifer, is to let the fairies out). Bake for 30 minutes. Check it at this point by tapping its bottom – if it sounds crisp and hollow, and the centre of the cross looks cooked, then it's done. If not, give it a little longer. Cool on a wire rack.

This will be a good-sized loaf, but you'll probably finish it in about half an hour…You can also freeze it for up to 3 months.

BREAKFASTS FOR SPRING

I am a great believer in breakfast. That said, by the time I get around to eating it I have usually been up for a good couple of hours, feeding animals and walking dogs, by which time I'm so hungry I could eat my own arm. There are times though when I have to grab breakfast soon after I get up – in which case I might just have an apple with Marmite. Don't knock it until you've tried it.

Apple & Marmite

1 apple   a jar of Marmite

Serves 1

Cut the apple into quarters and take out the core (these get saved for the pigs, who love them). Spread the apple quarters with Marmite as liberally as you like. Personally, I don't think you can ever have too much of the stuff.

Peanut butter is also delicious with apples. I would always go for crunchy, but you may disagree. Incidentally, you can make peanut butter surprisingly easily. I remember being round at a friend's house after school and her mum making it for us. It was like watching a magic trick. She put peanuts in a food processor, whizzed them up – noisily – and they turned into peanut butter. Just like that. So here's how to do it, should the mood take you.

Homemade Peanut Butter

300g (10½oz) raw peanuts
salt

groundnut oil

Makes 1 jar
Preheat your oven to 200°C (400°F), Gas Mark 6. Spread out the peanuts in a roasting tin and roast them for about 10–15 minutes until they are brown. Transfer them to a food processor, add a generous pinch of salt and blitz. At first they will just go crumbly. Have faith. The oil in the peanuts will soon start to release and before long you will have peanut butter. You may need to add a teaspoon or so of oil if you want a smoother peanut butter – do it gradually until you have the consistency you like. Scrape it out with a spatula and store in a clean jar or airtight container. It will keep in your fridge for 2–3 months.

Peanut butter is one of those recipes that you can endlessly tinker with, too. It's lovely using half and half peanuts and almonds. Personally I would never go down the chocolate peanut butter route, but there are no rules to say you can't…

More Substantial Spring Breakfasts

One of the many joys of keeping hens and ducks is that most days we have eggs so fresh they are still warm. I will sing the praises of duck eggs later (and there will be much singing) but the following recipes use hen eggs. Oh, and just a quick thing about eggs. They shouldn't be kept in the fridge. Just keep them in a bowl or on a rack out in the kitchen – where they'll last for at least four weeks.

Scromlette

Many years ago Ludo and I went to stay with our friends Zoran and Zvesta in Ljubljana in what was then still Yugoslavia. Zoran met us off the plane and drove us at his customary breakneck speed back to their apartment in the heart of the city. Zvesta, an extremely beautiful and successful actress, whom I was rather in awe of, met us at the door waving a wooden spoon. 'I'm making scromlette!' she announced.

Zvesta's scromlette has become something of a staple in our house. It is – as it sounds – a glorious hybrid of an omelette and scrambled eggs. It's quick, endlessly adaptable, can be eaten at any time of day and at any time of year. There are no careful quantities needed here – nothing can go wrong. It is one of those lovely dishes that can be made entirely to your own taste. This is the version I made this morning.

4–6 eggs (depending on how hungry you are)
feta cheese
a few sprigs of parsley, chopped
rapeseed or olive oil

1 or 2 tomatoes, chopped
1 red chilli, sliced
a generous handful of spinach
salt and pepper

Serves 2

Break the eggs (2 or 3 per person) into a bowl and whisk. Season with salt and pepper. Crumble in the feta – as much as you like or have left in the fridge. (I had a bit of leftover parsley as well, which I added to the eggs.)

Heat a little oil in the bottom of a frying pan over a medium heat then fry the tomatoes and chilli until soft – a few minutes. Add the spinach and let it wilt.

Pour in the eggs and feta and stir gently with a wooden spoon to combine the veg. Let it sit for a bit until it has cooked to the consistency you like your eggs. Stir again and it's ready.

Have it on or with toast, or a chunk of Soda Bread (see page 18), or with a slice of ham or just on its own. You can use any veg – Zvesta made hers with tomatoes, courgettes and peppers – any herbs, any cheese or no cheese. If you're having it for lunch or supper, it is delicious with a simple green salad.

Boiled Eggs & Asparagus

The Wye Valley where we live is one of the parts of the UK synonymous with asparagus. I assumed this was because of some ancient tradition, but no. It is actually something that began on a local farm less than 20 years ago. This farm has been in the same family for three generations and supplies fruit and vegetables to the surrounding area and beyond. It was the father of the current farmer who thought the sandy soil and sheltered, sloping fields would be ideal for asparagus and so it proved. A bit of savvy marketing on his part, and Wye Valley asparagus became 'a thing'. Which is wonderful, as far as I'm concerned, because I love the stuff and knowing it is grown practically on the doorstep is even better.

I can eat asparagus by the plateful – lightly steamed so the stalks still have a bit of crunch, with lemon, black pepper and lots of salty butter. But there can be no better start to a day than a decorative spear of asparagus dripping with the

Steamed asparagus

golden yolk of a perfectly boiled egg. And yes, your pee might smell funny for the rest of the day, but who cares?

1–2 eggs

5–10 asparagus spears, thick ends
  of the stalks removed

salt and pepper

Serves 1

Put a pan of water on to boil for the eggs and another for the asparagus. Put a pinch of salt in each pan. Once the water is boiling, lower your eggs (1 or 2 per person) gently into the water and set a timer for 4 minutes – for a medium-sized egg this will give you a nicely soft-boiled centre, perfect for dipping.

At the same time, put your asparagus spears (5 per egg) in their pan, or use a steamer if you have one. Once the eggs have had their time, take them out of the water and transfer to egg cups. Check the thickest part of the asparagus with the point of a knife. You don't want it too soft – like spaghetti it is best a little al dente. It should be done in pretty much the same time as your eggs. Drain and serve alongside the eggs with salt and a good grind of pepper.

Labneh with Radishes, Mint, Flatbreads & Za'atar

I delight in food that is designed to be eaten with your fingers, or scooped up with bread or rice, and mezze – the small dishes associated with Middle Eastern cuisine (which I love) – is just that sort of food. This breakfast is a homage to Mohammed and Marguerite, the wonderfully kind and hospitable friends of a friend, with whom we stayed when travelling in Jordan. Our days with them always started with a breakfast like this, usually outside, accompanied by small, thick glasses of mint tea.

You can recreate this breakfast (and imagine the warm rays of the Jordanian sun on your face as you eat it) simply by assembling various elements that you can buy ready-made. Labneh is just thick Greek yogurt that has been drained of all its liquid over 24 hours or so until it becomes like a cream or curd cheese. Regular cream cheese or quark will be a perfect substitute, drizzled with olive oil and sprinkled with za'atar, which is readily available in the spice aisles of supermarkets. Add pitta bread, radishes, mint – or cucumber, tomatoes, parsley – or all of those things. Walnut halves are a nice addition on the side. Turn it into lunch by adding a bowl of hummus too. And olives (if you are really that way inclined). But if you're in the mood, and you want to make all or some of these elements yourself, here's how.

Labneh

A quick note: labneh will keep in your fridge for two weeks if you form it into balls and store in an airtight jar covered with extra virgin olive oil. So choose the amount of yogurt to start with depending on what you want to do with it.

500g (1lb 2oz) thick Greek yogurt   1 teaspoon salt

Serves 4

Put the yogurt in a bowl. Add the salt and stir. Spoon the salted yogurt into a muslin-lined sieve or a muslin bag (available online) and suspend the sieve or bag over a bowl in your fridge for 24–48 hours. That's all you have to do. Store as suggested above, or put in a bowl, drizzle with olive oil and sprinkle with Za'atar.

Za'atar

1 tablespoon cumin seeds

1 tablespoon coriander seeds

2 tablespoons sesame seeds

2 tablespoons dried oregano or
   thyme (or a mixture)

2 tablespoons sumac

½ teaspoon sea salt flakes

½ teaspoon chilli flakes (if you
   like a bit of kick – but entirely
   optional)

Makes 1 small jar

Dry-roast the cumin and coriander seeds in a small saucepan until they start to become fragrant. Tip them into a pestle and mortar and grind them to a powder. Dry-roast the sesame seeds in the same pan until they just start to colour. Mix the ground cumin, coriander and the toasted sesame seeds with all the other ingredients and, once cool, store in an airtight jar for up to a month.

Flatbreads

There are lots of recipes out there for flatbreads. Some use yeast, some use yogurt, but the one I use – because it is so quick and easy and unfaffy – is Kate Colquhoun's recipe for Emergency Bread. I love Kate, and her brilliant *The Thrifty Cookbook* is one of my kitchen staples.

250g (9oz) plain flour, plus extra
   for dusting
1 teaspoon salt

1 tablespoon olive oil, plus extra for
   drizzling and greasing
150ml (¼ pint) water
sea salt flakes and pepper

Makes 4

Preheat your oven to 200°C (400°C), Gas Mark 6. Sift the flour into a bowl, add the salt and mix in well then add the oil. Pour about two-thirds of the water into the flour, mixing all the time. Continue to add water until you have a dough that holds together and doesn't stick to the sides of the bowl. It shouldn't be sloppy or wet.

Sprinkle a board or your worktop with flour and tip out the dough. Roughly knead it for a couple of minutes until the dough becomes stretchy and elastic. You can either divide it into 4 portions and roll each out until about 3mm (⅛in) thick, or roll out the whole lot and cook it whole (to share, ripping off bits as you need them). Or you could cut the dough into strips or whatever shape you like.

Drizzle the dough with a bit of olive oil, scatter with sea salt flakes, a grind of pepper or any seasoning you like (chilli flakes, dried herbs…) and put on a lightly oiled baking tray. Cook for 5–7 minutes until it is just starting to turn pale golden brown.

Mint Tea

Authentic Middle Eastern tea, served in small glasses in souks and cafés, is sweet, fragrant, refreshing and addictive. I could drink it all day, but I'd probably have no teeth left. Also, to make it properly, you need a tea pot that can sit on a stove or a flame, because you have to boil the tea. Pour enough boiling water into a tea pot over a tablespoon of tea leaves (gunpowder tea is ideal) to just cover them. Swirl it around, tip it out, then pour more water onto the soaked leaves, add sugar and boil them together in the pot for about five minutes. Add lots of fresh mint, boil for another couple of minutes, then it is ready to pour into glasses from a suitably showy height. It's one of those drinks, I think (like a really good cocktail), that tastes so good because someone else has done all the hard work to make it.

Simpler, infinitely quicker and not as teeth rotting, is to put a bunch of mint in a tea pot, pour over boiling water and let it sit for a bit before pouring. I'll sometimes add a slice of lemon to my mug for a bit of summery, citrus zing.

MAIN COURSES FOR SPRING

꩜

The recipes that follow are a bit of a mixture. Some are truly seasonal, relying on ingredients that can only be gathered in the spring, like wild garlic and fresh hawthorn leaves, but most of these dishes can be cooked at any time of year. Some are lighter and almost summery, others – like the split pea and ham soup – are my go-tos for a cold day when I need something that will properly warm my bones.

Cooking a Ham

꩜

I don't know why, but until very recently I thought that cooking a ham was not something a mere mortal could do. I imagined it was extraordinarily complicated, which is why most of us buy hams ready-cooked and glazed at Christmas and then revert to shop-bought, pre-sliced stuff for the rest of the year. So it was something of a revelation when I discovered how easy it is to cook a ham and – even more gratifying – how many things you can do with it for many days afterwards. Nor does it need to be eaten in a room decked out with tinsel and fairy lights to taste good. A ham, dear friends, can be for any time, not just for Christmas…

You start with a joint of gammon – smoked or unsmoked, on or off the bone, it makes no difference to the way you cook it. If you've never done it before and you're a bit nervous about mucking it up (you won't, but I know I was), start with a smaller joint – something around a kilo (2lb 4oz) in weight which will happily feed four people with some leftovers, or two people with lots of leftovers. It's worth bearing in mind that you are going to cook this initially in a pot on the hob, so you need a pot big enough to fit it in.

Weigh your gammon and work out how long you need to cook it for. Here's what you need to know to do the maths:

❅ Cook for 20 minutes per 450g (1lb) PLUS an extra 20 minutes.

❅ Boil it for half that time.

❅ Roast it for the other half.

So a 1.35kg (3lb) gammon needs to cook for 1 hour and 20 minutes (boil for 40 minutes, roast for 40 minutes).

Put the gammon in its pot and then decide what liquid you want to add. It can just be water – ideally enough to cover it, but don't worry if your pan isn't quite big enough to allow this to happen. You can just turn the gammon half way through the cooking process. Water is one option, but I've also done this very successfully with apple juice, a mix of apple juice and cranberry juice (which is quite Christmassy) and cider (probably my favourite). Nigella Lawson caused a sensation in her book *How to Eat* (a copy of which I was given on my 30th

birthday and I have used pretty constantly ever since) when suggesting cooking a ham in Coca-Cola. The results are, according to my friend Lucy, magnificent.

Whatever your liquid, you might want to throw in some seasonings – an onion cut into quarters, a few peppercorns, a bay leaf or two – and then you bring the liquid to the boil and let your gammon simmer happily in its fragrant bath, transforming, as it does so, into a ham. Meanwhile, preheat your oven to 180°C (350°F), Gas Mark 4.

When it has had its time, lift the ham out of the cooking liquid (WHICH I URGE YOU NOT TO THROW AWAY! You've just made the best stock ever without even thinking about it. Set it aside to cool, then refrigerate or freeze to use as a base for soup later – see page 41) and put it in a foil-lined roasting tin. Remove the skin from the top of the meat, leaving the layer of fat beneath it. Score the fat in a diamond pattern, if you like, then cover the meat with foil and put in the oven.

Glazes for ham

About 20 minutes before the ham is ready, remove the foil covering and brush it with a glaze – you can use all sorts of things here. My lovely neighbour Jo makes membrillo from her quince trees, which is delicious with cheese and cold meats (see page 173). She's baked cakes with it, but it is also an excellent glaze for a ham. Maple syrup and grainy mustard is a classic one, as is marmalade or apricot jam. I tried it once with a crab apple and chilli jelly (another present from Jo), which was spectacular. If you're using some sort of jam or jelly, warm it up so it is runny, then you can spoon or brush it onto your ham more easily. Return the joint to the oven and leave it to cook for its remaining time uncovered.

Red cabbage

It is now ready to eat. Hot, straight from the oven, I like it with mashed butternut squash, Savoy cabbage steamed in a little butter with caraway seeds, leeks braised in white wine, or red cabbage cooked in a low oven for about an hour with finely chopped onions and apple, a bit of sugar and cider vinegar.

Then – if you haven't polished it all off in one sitting – you have the almost infinite joy that leftover ham can bring. So, if you are going to cook a ham, always plan to cook more than you need for one meal. Cold hunks of home-cooked ham can be the basis for the quickest, simplest, most satisfying of meals. Hard to beat is a plate of ham with a baked potato (better still, a baked sweet potato: rub the skin with a little oil and flaked salt, prick it with the point of a knife a few times and cook at 200°C/400°F/Gas Mark 6 until soft) and a salad or a crunchy homemade slaw. Shredded white cabbage, grated carrot, maybe an apple too, mixed with rocket or chopped flat leaf parsley, a few raisins and walnuts or cashews, if you like, lightly dressed with oil, lemon juice and grainy mustard is a good one.

Baked sweet potato

Crunchy slaw

As is a ham sandwich, like this one, made with super-easy, super-quick (and a little bit surprising) homemade bread and (in my opinion) one of the finest pickles ever invented.

A Ham Sandwich on Beer Bread with Piccalilli

I had one of my best jobs ever when I was 19, driving the supply truck for an African safari company. It took me to some of the wildest, most remote parts of the continent. We camped out, falling asleep to the sound of roaring lions and waking to find baboons trying to raid our supplies. All our cooking was done on fires and we had to be entirely self-sufficient for weeks as there were no shops nearby. Rick, my co-driver, one evening as the fire was dying down, tipped half a bag of flour into one of the cast iron Dutch ovens we used, added some salt and then solemnly poured in a can of beer. I thought he'd gone mad. 'You wait,' he said. He put the pot on the dying embers of the fire, piled more on the lid and went to bed. The next morning, as I crawled out of my tent at dawn, Rick waved me over to the fire and lifted the lid of the pot. Inside was a perfect loaf of bread. I looked at him like a kid who has just watched a magic trick. 'Beer,' he said, smiling, 'miraculous stuff. Now you can make the coffee.'

You can use lager or bitter or stout for this bread – whatever beer you like. All work and all give their own flavour and colour to the loaf.

Caraway Beer Bread

375g (13oz) self-raising flour

1 teaspoon salt

2 teaspoons caraway seeds

330ml (11fl oz) beer

oil for greasing

Makes 1 loaf

Preheat your oven to 180°C (350°F), Gas Mark 4. Mix the flour, salt and caraway seeds in a bowl. Pour in the beer and stir with a spoon until everything is incorporated and you have a sticky dough. Transfer to a greased 900-g (2-lb) loaf tin. Cook for 50–60 minutes, then check to see if it's cooked by inserting a skewer (it should come out clean) and/or give its bottom a little tap to see if it sounds crisp and hollow. Cool on a wire rack.

WARNING: Making beer bread can become a tiny bit addictive, because it is so easy and so adaptable. You can use different beers and different flavourings. You can add cheese or nuts, or anything you like really. Like soda bread. And every bit as moreish.

Piccalilli

I love this bright yellow mustard pickle. I was indoctrinated at a young age by my grandmother, Paddy, who also loved piccalilli and would have it with everything. Ludo hates it. His ham sandwich will be eaten with English mustard and lashings of mayo (from the large squeezy bottle in the fridge).

I planned to include a recipe for piccalilli here and asked my friend Angharad – or Rag, as she is fondly known – if she had one she was willing to share. Angharad is our local Queen of Preserves and her products have garnered her many well-deserved awards. She will crop up throughout this book, because if ever I want to make something jammy or pickley, it is her brain I pick. However, as far as piccalilli is concerned, she couldn't help. This was her reply to my request for a recipe: 'I made piccalilli once and it was a disaster! After swearing profusely, I vowed not to make it again!' My feeling is that if Rag can't make it, I certainly can't, so I will continue – guilt-free – to buy piccalilli made by someone else and relish every tangy, yellow mouthful.

Once you have all the component parts for your sandwich, it is simply a matter of assembly. I like this as an open sandwich, beer bread sliced, smeared with salty butter, topped with thick bits of ham and a good dollop of beautiful, golden piccalilli. And alongside, some crispy leaves of Little Gem, or a handful of rocket or watercress, because the green goes so beautifully with the pink of the ham and the yellow of the pickle. And a big mug of tea.

That Ham Stock

I'm sorry I got a bit shouty on page 36 about not throwing the stock away, but you will thank me, I promise, because it makes the most fantastic, flavoursome base for so many soups, particularly root vegetable soups – celeriac, chestnut and apple; swede, parsnip and carrot. But for me, it is the perfect excuse to make this – a meal I love so much, it is in my Top 10 of Last Suppers…

Swedish Yellow Split Pea Soup

I first ate this while working on a ship in Norway. The crew (including, importantly, the cook) was predominantly Swedish so it was this soup that was served on Thursdays. I never quite established why Thursdays and not another day, but it is traditionally eaten with crispbread, Västerbotten cheese and a sweet, mild mustard called Slotts Senap, which is added to the soup as you eat.

There are various recipes for this soup to be found, but this one comes courtesy of my dear – and thoroughly Swedish – friend Anders. He comes from a farming family which has lived in the village of Nås for 400 years. This is the very simple recipe that has been passed down his family for generations. So it is probably as authentic as you can get. And absolutely delicious – or, as Anders would say – 'scrumptious'.

500g (1lb 2oz) yellow split peas
2 litres (3½ pints) ham stock
300g (10½oz) ham
1 onion, finely chopped

a few sprigs of thyme (or
  ½ teaspoon dried thyme)
1 bay leaf

Serves 4

Soak the yellow split peas in lots of water overnight. Remove the dried floating shells and then drain. (Not all yellow peas need soaking, so you might be able to miss this bit out – check the instructions on the packet.)

Put your delicious ham stock into a big pot with the peas, the ham (cut or shredded into good-sized chunks), the onion, thyme and bay leaf. Bring to the boil, remove the foam that forms on the surface, and then let it gently simmer for 3 hours, stirring occasionally. If the soup is too thick, you can add water to get the consistency you like, but Anders's family likes it fairly thick, as do I. More stew than soup.

More Soups for Spring

On the subject of soup, here are another couple of favourites that I cook a lot at this time of year, because they are warming and substantial but also feel fresh and sort of 'springy'.

Miso Soup
with Noodles & Greens

This is more suggestion than recipe, because you can use whatever noodles you like and whatever green veg you might have to hand. This soup is quick and easy, and I often make it and put it in a food flask to take with me if I'm working away from home. It is perfect for those spring days that feel like winter and you just want something warm, soothing and restorative. And you don't have to stick to just veg. Both chicken and prawns work well in this soup. Either cook some raw, thinly sliced chicken with the garlic and ginger, or add pre-cooked or leftover chicken just before you add the veg. If you go for prawns, add them at this point too.

I like to use soba or thin rice noodles that come in blocks. I prefer white miso as it is a little lighter in taste, but brown miso also works well. My favourite veg for this are baby corn, sugarsnap peas and pak choi. Amounts are up to you, but I might use two or three baby corn, split in half, six sugarsnaps and one sliced pak choi. Use as much chilli you like and include the seeds if you like the heat.

1 portion of noodles

rapeseed oil

toasted sesame oil (optional)

1 garlic clove, sliced or grated

1 thumb-sized piece of ginger, peeled and sliced into matchsticks or grated

½ small carrot, cut into matchsticks

1 red chilli, sliced thinly (optional)

300ml (½ pint) stock (vegetable or chicken, fresh or from a cube)

a mix of veg

1 tablespoon miso paste

100ml (3½fl oz) boiling water

1 spring onion, sliced thinly

a small bunch of fresh coriander, roughly chopped

juice of 1 lime

soy sauce

Serves 1

Cook the noodles according to the instructions on the packet, then drain, cool in cold water to stop the cooking process, drain again and leave aside.

Heat a splash of rapeseed oil, or a mix of rapeseed and toasted sesame oil, in a wok or saucepan over a medium heat. Add the garlic and ginger and push them around in the oil, being careful the garlic doesn't catch and burn. Add the carrot matchsticks and let them sweat in the oil for a few minutes and then add the chilli if you're using it. Give everything a minute or so more in the oil, gently pushing it around, before adding the stock. Bring it to the boil then simmer gently for 5 minutes or so, until the carrots have softened a bit and the stock has been infused with the flavours of the garlic, ginger and chilli.

Now add the veg in the order of the cooking time it needs. If you are using my favourites, the corn goes first, then a couple of minutes later the sugarsnaps and the crisp ends of the pak choi. Don't add the pak choi leaves yet.

Dissolve the miso paste in the boiling water, then add it to the soup. Stir so that its grainy cloudiness is well distributed, then take the pan off the heat. The miso is added at this stage, rather than at the beginning, because if you boil miso you risk damaging its flavour and health benefits. Add the pak choi leaves, half the spring onion and half the coriander.

Put your cooked noodles into a warm, generous-sized bowl. Ladle over the vegetable miso soup, scatter it with the remaining spring onion and coriander, add a good squeeze of fresh lime juice and a shake of soy sauce.

Spring in Your Step Soup

It is, of course, an amazing luxury to live the way most of us do these days, with food from all over the world available at almost every time of year. But although few of us rely on Nature's bounty to sustain us throughout the year, it is worth bearing in mind that, at certain times of year, Nature does provide us with exactly what we need. And in spring, that thing is nettles.

Contained in those unfriendly stinging leaves is a cornucopia of vitamins and minerals, including vitamins A and D, iron and potassium. They are, according to my forager friend Liz Knight, one of the most nutritious, complete foods on the planet. Exactly what we need when we are emerging from the rigours of a cold, dark winter.

First find your nettle patch! For this soup, select the young, fresh, small leaves at the tops of the stems and cut them off with a pair of scissors. To avoid being stung, wear washing-up gloves or gardening gloves. Try to pick from different patches, rather than harvesting everything from the same spot – it is

good foraging practice to pick a few leaves and then move on to another patch. Ideally, it shouldn't be obvious where you have taken your harvest from.

For this recipe you need about one-third of a carrier bag of nettles.

olive oil

25g (1oz) butter

1 onion, chopped

1 leek, finely sliced

1 large floury potato (like a Maris Piper), scrubbed and cut into cubes

a handful of kale leaves, removed from the tough stalks and chopped

1 litre (1¾ pints) vegetable stock (fresh or from a cube)

100g (3½oz) baby spinach leaves

50g (1¾oz) young nettle leaves, stems removed, washed

a grating of nutmeg (optional)

salt and pepper

Serves 4

Heat a good glug of olive oil with the butter in a large saucepan. Add the onion and leek with a good pinch of salt and sweat over a medium heat for about 10 minutes until both are soft and the onion is translucent. Add the potato, kale and stock, put a lid on the pot and bring to the boil. Then reduce to a simmer and cook for 10–15 minutes until the potato is soft.

Add the spinach and nettle leaves and cook until wilted (it will take barely a minute).

Remove from the heat and blitz the soup until smooth. Season with black pepper, a grating of nutmeg, if you like, and maybe more salt.

Delicious topped with grated Parmesan or pecorino and croûtons (which *Croûtons* you can buy or make, either by drizzling a chunky slice of bread – sourdough is good – with olive oil and letting it crisp up in the oven or, even easier, over-cooking a bit of toast and crumbling it up on the soup). Or in late spring, a blob of Wild Garlic Pesto (see page 54) drizzled on the top of the soup is amazing.

Spring Veg with Herbs & Feta

There are days, particularly in the spring and summer, when I have an irrepressible craving for a big bowl of green veg, lightly steamed, drizzled when warm with really good olive oil, spritzed with lemon, scattered with herbs. It feels like eating all the vitamins you will ever need at once, but in a way that is gloriously simple and deeply pleasurable. This is less a recipe, more a suggestion. Use any veg you like and adorn it as little or as much as your craving demands!

Lightly steam a mix of green veg – broccoli, asparagus, broad beans, French beans, peas, spinach, courgettes. Don't stint on the amount – remember this is not a side dish (although it can be) – and steam until the vegetables are only just cooked and no more. You want to retain a bit of bite.

Pile onto a plate or into a bowl and drizzle with oil. You could use a flavoured oil – walnut or chilli, for example – or just a fruity, unctuous extra virgin olive oil. You could, at this point, just scatter over a good mixed handful of roughly chopped herbs – anything you like or have handy – parsley, basil, mint, coriander, chives – grind over some black pepper and sprinkle with sea salt flakes and eat.

Or you can make the dish a tiny bit less Spartan by spritzing it with a good squirt of fresh lemon juice and adding a crumble of feta over the vegetables, or using a vegetable peeler to shave wide curls of Parmesan to top them with. Toasted seeds are a nice addition too – dry-fry a tablespoon of pumpkin and sunflower seeds and sprinkle them over. But whatever you do, this is a beautiful plate of food that you can rustle up in not much more time than it takes to make a sandwich.

Smoked Fish Kedgeree
with Peas, Parsley & Chives

Kedgeree seems to be one of those dishes that has rather fallen out of fashion, relegated to the occasional mention in a period drama. 'Pondlebury, would you ask cook to send up a dish of kedgeree. Lord Banderhay can't abide devilled kidneys and will be insufferable until lunchtime.'

But you don't need a butler or a peerage to enjoy kedgeree, and you don't have to eat it for breakfast. I love it for lunch, piled up in a big dish for everyone to help themselves. Although there looks like a lot of prep to do, much of it can be done in advance and is not very onerous. Then it is just a matter of putting everything together once the rice is cooked and everyone is ready to eat.

500g (1lb 2oz) skin-on smoked
   haddock fillet
1 lemon
1 bay leaf
a few peppercorns
2 eggs
200g (7oz) peas (fresh or frozen)
a handful each of parsley and chives

50g (1¾oz) raw cashew nuts
   (optional)
1 onion
oil
1–2 tablespoons curry paste
300g (10½oz) basmati rice
25g (1oz) butter
salt and pepper

Serves 4

This first bit can all be done in advance. Put the fish in a deep frying pan or saucepan. If it is one big fillet and won't fit, simply cut it in half. Cut a couple of slices from the lemon and add them, along with the bay leaf and the peppercorns, to the pan. Pour over enough boiling water to cover the fillet and simmer until the fish is cooked – which will take about 5 minutes. It will start to separate into big flakes. Remove the fish from the poaching liquid. Sieve the poaching liquid into a jug and reserve. Once the fish is cool, peel away the skin and discard, then break up the fish into large flakes.

Put the eggs in a small saucepan of boiling water. Boil for 10 minutes if you want them properly hard-boiled, but I like them to still have slightly runny yolks, so tend to do them for about 7 minutes. Once done, take them out of the pan and cool them under cold running water for a minute or put them in a bowl of ice water. This helps to prevent dark rings forming around the yolks. Once cool, peel and cut them into halves or quarters and set aside.

Plunge the peas into a pan of boiling water and cook for 30 seconds or so, then drain, refresh under cold water and set aside. Chop the parsley and chives. Toast the cashews (if using) in a dry pan until they brown, then tip out onto a dish to cool.

Squeeze the juice of the remaining lemon and reserve.

When you are ready to cook, dice the onion, then heat a good glug of oil in a large saucepan or casserole over a medium heat. Add the onion and a good pinch of salt and cook until soft and translucent.

Add the curry paste – the more you use the stronger the flavour – and stir over the heat until it coats the onion. Tip in the rice and stir so it, too, is well mixed with the onion and curry paste. Then add enough poaching liquid so it comes to about 2cm (¾in) above the level of the rice in the pan and bring to a boil.

Keep an eye on your rice – you want it to retain a bit of bite and the grains to remain fluffy and not become a solid mass. If you need more liquid, add a little more poaching liquid or use boiling water.

Once the rice is cooked, turn the heat down low and add the butter, lemon juice, peas and the fish. Stir gently to heat through, trying not to break up the fish too much. Add half the chopped herbs, a good pinch of sea salt flakes and a grinding of pepper. Stir again gently so everything is combined.

Tip it into a warmed serving dish, top with the eggs and scatter with the remaining herbs and the cashew nuts. I like kedgeree with a crunchy green salad alongside it – sliced Little Gems, watercress, celery and cucumber, something like that – lightly dressed with just oil and lemon juice and seasoned with salt and pepper. A hunk of this season's Soda Bread (see page 18) wouldn't go amiss either.

Crunchy green salad

Wild Garlic Time

There is that wonderful moment, just when we need it most, when the first small-but-oh-so-welcome signs of spring start to appear. The snowdrops bloom, a shy yellow primrose unfurls in the shelter of a hedge. By March, bright yellow celandines pop up along sunny banks and verges and jewel-like spots of colour peep out from the leaf litter in the woods – wood anemones, violets, the first green leaves that are the precursor to the glorious spectacle that is bluebell season.

And this is also the time when clusters of deep emerald leaves will start to emerge at the foot of the still-bare oak and beech trees, quickly spreading to cover the forest floor in a lush, potently fragrant carpet. This is wild garlic, and we are lucky that it grows in profusion in most of our neighbouring woods, because it is an edible seasonal treat that I look forward to every year. As the days get warmer, its distinctive garlicky smell gets stronger. Thin stalks start to sprout from among the leaves, topped with spear-like buds which burst into a pompom of white flowers. These are also edible and will decorate salads and vegetable dishes, be mixed into scrambled eggs and garnish soups. The leaves can be used in a myriad of ways, but as synonymous with spring as lambing and sowing the first vegetable seeds, is the making of wild garlic pesto.

Wild Garlic Pesto

100g (3½oz) wild garlic leaves
(about 2 generous handfuls),
washed and dried
50g (1¾oz) blanched hazelnuts,
toasted

50g (1¾oz) hard cheese, grated
zest of 1 unwaxed lemon, plus
a squeeze of juice
olive oil
salt and pepper

Makes 1 large jar

Place the wild garlic leaves, nuts, cheese and lemon zest into a food processor and blitz until chopped. Taste, then add a squeeze of lemon juice along with a bit of salt and pepper to season. Pulse to mix. With the motor running, pour olive oil into the bowl of the food processor until you reach a pesto consistency. Taste and adjust the seasoning if necessary. It may need an extra squeeze of lemon juice too.

Transfer the pesto to a clean jam jar and pour a little extra oil over the top of the pesto to cover it and make it airtight. Store in the fridge for up to 2 weeks, or put it in a plastic tub and freeze for up to 12 months.

Wild garlic pesto is delicious on pasta just as basil pesto is, but like basil pesto, it also works with lots of other dishes. A spoonful mixed with more lemon juice and a bit of oil makes a beautiful dressing on a plate of sliced tomatoes, or can be drizzled over a tomato bruschetta. It's lovely as an alternative to mint sauce with lamb. Then there's chicken.

Wild garlic-dressed tomatoes

This chicken dish, all cooked in one roasting tin, uses both wild garlic leaves and the pesto and is a wonderful showcase for both and a perfect supper for a spring weekend. I'd serve it with a big salad of mixed leaves and a plate of tomatoes, dressed with wild garlic pesto dressing. It might be overkill to try a soda bread with wild garlic – or, indeed, a garlic bread using wild garlic in the butter – but the season is short, so make the most of it, I say!

Spring Chicken
with Wild Garlic & New Potatoes

6–8 skin-on, bone-in chicken
  thighs
3 tablespoons Wild Garlic Pesto
  (see above)
750g (1lb 10oz) new potatoes,
  scrubbed and halved or
  quartered

olive oil
2 handfuls of wild garlic leaves,
  any flowers reserved for garnish
150ml (¼ pint) dry white wine
200–250ml (7–9fl oz) chicken
  stock (fresh or from a cube)
salt and pepper

Serves 4

Open out the chicken thighs and spread the wild garlic pesto over the flesh side, avoiding the skin where possible. You can cook them straight away or leave them to marinate for up to 24 hours. Once ready to cook, preheat the oven to 200°C (400°F), Gas Mark 6.

Put the potatoes into a medium–large roasting tin big enough to hold the chicken thighs in a single layer. Drizzle with a little olive oil and season with salt and pepper. Push the wild garlic leaves in between the potatoes. Pour over the white wine and chicken stock – you need about 1cm (½in) of liquid in the bottom of the tin, so if your tin is large, you might need to add a bit more stock and/or wine. Then place the pesto-marinated chicken thighs on top of the potatoes and garlic leaves with the skin facing up. Drizzle with olive oil and season the skin with a few pinches of salt.

Bake for 40 minutes, or until the potatoes are tender and the chicken cooked through with crisp golden skin. Leave to rest for 5–10 minutes before serving with any wild garlic flowers scattered over the top.

Who Needs Parsley When You've Got Hawthorn?

It was Liz Knight who revealed to me that adding the fresh spring leaves of hawthorn to a dish is an excellent wild alternative to parsley. I met Liz at our local food festival where she was selling her wild and wonderful preserves, spice mixes and relishes. She is the first to admit that she gets most of her food at the supermarket like everyone else, but foraging gives her the huge pleasure of gathering wild, free ingredients to add to everyday dishes – like the nettles in the Spring in Your Step Soup on page 45. Her knowledge of wild plants, their uses and benefits is boundless, and every time I go foraging with her I discover something new, usually about a plant I am already familiar with. It was Liz who

told me not to spend hours digging up my ground elder. 'It was brought here by the Romans, because it is so good to eat.' It is too – use as you would spinach. And I had no idea that the fresh spring leaves of hawthorn are every bit as delicious as parsley. So I've used them in my favourite pasta dish – favourite not just because of the happy marriage of flavours between the crab, lemon and chilli, but because it is our campervan regular and will always be the dish that kicks off a holiday.

Linguine
with Crab, Chilli, Lemon, Rocket & Hawthorn

250g (9oz) dried linguine
1 garlic clove, finely chopped
½–1 long red chilli, finely chopped
150g (5½oz) fresh crabmeat (just white or a mixture of brown and white), or 1 can of crabmeat
zest of 1 unwaxed lemon, plus

a squeeze of juice (optional)
extra virgin olive oil
a small handful of hawthorn leaves or parsley, roughly chopped
2 handfuls of rocket
salt and pepper

Serves 2

Put a large saucepan of salted water on to boil and cook the linguine according to the packet instructions. While the pasta is cooking, mix together the garlic, chilli, crabmeat and lemon zest with a little olive oil in a large bowl, big enough to take all the pasta. Using tongs, remove the cooked pasta from the water and put straight into the large bowl with the crabmeat. Stir everything together really well to coat the pasta in the oily crab mixture. If necessary, add a couple of spoonfuls of pasta water and stir well until the pasta is coated in a silky sauce.

Season generously. Mix well and taste – it might benefit from a squeeze of lemon juice. Stir in the hawthorn leaves or parsley and rocket and serve.

Pretty & Pink – a Homage to Rhubarb

꒰꒱

Rhubarb is something that works beautifully in both sweet and savoury dishes. It is wonderful with pork – either made into a compote and served like apple sauce with a roast or chops, or roasted beneath a tenderloin that has been wrapped in thin, salty leaves of Parma ham. But for speed, flavour and all-round prettiness, try this:

Mackerel with Rhubarb

4–6 stalks of rhubarb, trimmed
1 orange
caster sugar
olive oil

4 skin-on mackerel fillets, bones
  removed
salt and pepper
watercress, to serve

Serves 2

Preheat your oven to 200°C (400°F), Gas Mark 6. Slice the rhubarb into 5cm (2in) lengths and place in a roasting tin. Zest the orange and sprinkle the zest over the rhubarb. Squeeze over the juice of half the orange and sprinkle with a couple of good pinches of sugar. Roast for 7–10 minutes until the rhubarb is soft but still holds it shape. Remove from the oven, leaving in the tin.

Turn your grill to its highest setting. Take your mackerel fillets, put a couple of slashes in the skin, drizzle with olive oil and season with salt and pepper. Place them, skin side up, on top of the rhubarb and put the tin under the grill for about 5 minutes until the mackerel is cooked. Divide the rhubarb between 2 plates, top with the mackerel fillets and pour over any juices from the roasting tin. Serve with a handful of watercress alongside and eat immediately.

Mr Brock & His Ice Creams

Mr Brock – AKA Freddie – lives in a house on the opposite side of the River Wye from me. He is a connoisseur of ice cream and how to make it, which given that he is 12 years old, is no small achievement. I spent a very happy afternoon in his kitchen getting a master class in ice cream-making and came away with four of his favourite seasonal recipes which he has given me permission to share with you. His ethos is to make ice cream with as local ingredients as possible. He uses milk and cream from the local dairy farm down the road and seasonal flavours that can be picked or scrumped from his garden or those of his neighbours. Apart from chocolate. Which comes from the village shop.

A couple of things to note before you start. Freddie advocates that you make your ice cream base on one day, chill it overnight and then churn it the next – so you might want to plan ahead (The base of all Mr Brock's ice creams is the custard described opposite.) All these recipes require an ice cream-maker and a thermometer. If you don't keep the bowl of your ice cream-maker in the freezer all the time, make sure you don't forget to put it in well before you plan to make your ice cream.

Rhubarb, Honey & Ginger Ice Cream
A Mr Brock Bestseller

You can make the rhubarb purée for this ice ceam in advance – a day ahead if you like. It seems like a lot of rhubarb, but Freddie tried this recipe with half the amount, and he said it was too creamy and not rhubarby enough.

FOR THE CUSTARD BASE
6 egg yolks (save the whites to make meringues)
200g (7oz) caster sugar

3 tablespoons skimmed milk powder
1 litre (1¾ pints) whole milk
150ml (¼ pint) double cream

Serves 8–10

Whisk the egg yolks, sugar and skimmed milk powder until smooth and pale. Put the milk and the cream in a pan and heat until bubbles form at the side but it doesn't actually boil. Take the pan off the heat and pour it into the egg mixture. Have your pot-washer thoroughly clean the pan while you stir. Then pour the mixture back into the pan and warm over a gentle heat until it reaches 75°C (167°F). Take it off the heat and let it cool. In the meantime, make your rhubarb purée.

FOR THE RHUBARB PURÉE
1.2kg (2lb 12oz) rhubarb
2 thumb-sized pieces of ginger, peeled and grated

1 teaspoon ground ginger
8 tablespoons honey
juice of ½ orange
ginger wine (optional)

Preheat the oven to 200°C (400°F), Gas Mark 6. Trim the rhubarb and cut into chunks. Put it in a roasting tin with all the other ingredients (except the ginger wine, if using) and cook for 40 minutes, until the rhubarb is soft. Let it cool and then blend to a smooth, thick purée. Freddie uses a Nutribullet for this and it does make amazingly smooth purées (and is easy to wash up, which is a bonus if you are Freddie's pot-washer).

If you like ginger wine and happen to have a bottle, stir a glug into your custard base once it is cool, then add the rhubarb purée and transfer it all to the fridge overnight, or at least for a few hours. This, Freddie tells me, is to allow the flavours to properly develop and for the custard to continue to thicken.

The next day, pour your lovely, rhubarby, gingery custard into the bowl of your ice cream-maker and churn until it has become softly frozen. Scoop out with a spatula into a tub and store in the freezer. Take it out and put in the fridge about 30 minutes before you want to eat it.

PUDDINGS FOR SPRING

I am not, I confess, much of a pudding person. I don't have a very sweet tooth and I don't want to have to rely on technical skills I absolutely do not have. The puddings that follow are not remotely elaborate or complicated, and offer a sweet, but not too sweet, end to a meal.

Self-saucing Pudding
with Orange & Lemon

It was my friend Lucy who introduced me to the concept of self-saucing puddings. She lived in Australia for a few years, where they are something of a staple pud, like crumble is for the British. On first appearance they look like a regular sponge pudding but dig beneath and you find a delicious pool of sauce. Most recipes use lemon, but I tried it out one evening using a combination of orange and lemon instead. It got the thumbs up, so here it is.

60g (2¼oz) butter, softened, plus
  extra for greasing
125g (4½ oz) golden caster sugar
zest and juice of 1 unwaxed lemon
zest of 1 unwaxed orange

2 eggs, separated
4 tablespoons self-raising flour
300ml (½ pint) whole milk
1 teaspoon caraway seeds, lightly
  toasted in a dry pan

Serves 4

Preheat your oven to 180°C (350°F), Gas Mark 4, and grease 4 large ovenproof ramekins with a little butter. Beat together the butter, sugar and the lemon and orange zest using an electric whisk until pale and creamy. Then beat in the egg yolks, one at a time. Fold in a spoonful of flour, followed by a bit of milk, and keep going until you have a smooth batter. Don't worry if the mixture looks as if it has split – this is normal. Add the lemon juice and stir everything together until combined.

Using clean beaters, whisk the egg whites until they form stiff peaks and fold them into the mixture. Then divide between the buttered ramekins. Put the ramekins in a roasting tin and pour in enough hot water to come half way up the sides of the ramekins. Bake in the oven for 25 minutes. The puddings will rise and their tops will turn a deep golden colour. When the puddings are ready, bring them out of the oven and let them cool for about 5 minutes or so before serving.

Foraging for Gorse

It was barely spring when my friend Liz Knight suggested we go and forage on the mountain behind her house. 'There'll be nothing to pick!' I objected, but I was wrong. Although the trees were still bare of leaves, the gorse was starting to flower – those small yellow blooms, startlingly bright in an otherwise colourless landscape. Liz uses gorse to make into syrup for wild piña coladas. As it was a rather damp, not very spring-like spring day, the idea of a bit of tropical frivolity was irresistible. But it was – she conceded – too cold for the gorse to be giving off its characteristic scent of coconut and honey, so we used the few blooms we picked to decorate piña coladas made with ready-infused rum. We drank them in her kitchen, looking out through the drizzle and tried to pretend her garden was a Caribbean beach...

Liz's Gorse Piña Coladas

You can buy ready-infused gorse rum – try Heath & Hedge Gorseflower White Rum, which is made in Dartmoor. But infusing rum only takes a couple of days (unlike making infused gins or vodkas, which takes months), so if you feel like giving it a go, this is how you do it.

Gorse-infused Rum

a large handful of gorse flowers (picked on a sunny morning)

350ml (12fl oz) white rum

1 heaped teaspoon sugar

Makes 350ml (12fl oz)

Put the gorse flowers in a Kilner jar, pour over the rum, add the sugar, seal and give it a bit of a shake. Leave in a cool, dark place for a couple of days, then strain and it is ready for drinking.

A traditional piña colada is made with rum, coconut cream and pineapple juice, but we left out the coconut cream, letting the gorse flowers in the rum do their thing. So Liz simply blitzed a good-sized chunk of fresh pineapple in a blender with ice and poured it over the gorse-infused rum. You don't need me to give you weights and measures. You know how strong you like your drinks.

As we were testing out the merits of gorse-infused rum, I had an idea that the coconutty fragrance of gorse might go well with chocolate. 'It would!' Liz said. 'I dry the flowers and use them in chocolate truffles. But there's also an amazing gorse chocolate made by a company called Chocolarder in Cornwall.' This was good news, because picking gorse is a pain (literally). If I could use ready-flavoured gorse chocolate, I thought, I could just use a few flowers for decoration. So here is a recipe for a very easy, partly foraged pudding, made even easier because someone else has done the bulk of the foraging for you…

Gorse Chocolate Mousse
with Coconut & Gorse Flowers

140g (5oz) gorse-flavoured
   chocolate, such as Chocolarder
   Wild Gorse Flower 50% Milk
   Chocolate
4 eggs

TO DECORATE
toasted coconut flakes
a few gorse flowers (about 12 – not
   too irksome a job!)

Serves 4

Put a heatproof bowl (Pyrex ones are good for this) over a pan of simmering water, making sure the bottom of the bowl doesn't touch the water. Break up the chocolate and put it in the bowl to melt gently over the heat. Stir as it starts to melt, then take it off the heat and keep stirring until it is totally melted. Take the bowl off the pan and set aside to cool for a bit.

Separate the eggs, putting the whites into a large, clean bowl. Whisk them into soft peaks. Beat the egg yolks just to break them up, then stir them into the melted chocolate until they are fully mixed in. Add a spoonful of your whipped egg whites to the chocolate mixture, then carefully fold the chocolate and the remaining egg whites together, trying to keep as much air in the mixture as possible.

Divide the mixture into 4 glasses or ramekins and leave in the fridge for 3 hours to set – but they'll keep for up to 48 hours (if you can wait that long). Once ready to eat, decorate with toasted coconut flakes and gorse flowers and serve immediately.

Frozen Yogurt Soufflé
with Ginger & Honey

If there can be such a thing as a soufflé that doesn't induce panic, this is it. Purists may scoff at the idea that this dish could be described as a soufflé, as it is not baked, but other than that, it has all the component parts of a soufflé without any possibility of it sagging in a thoroughly dispiriting fashion the moment you remove it from the oven. And its lovely fresh flavours of lemon, ginger and honey – all things I love – make it the perfect light, fresh end to a meal.

400ml (14fl oz) Greek yogurt
100g (3½oz) crème fraîche
zest and juice of 1 unwaxed lemon
2 tablespoons floral honey
   (something like lavender or
   heather)

3 balls of stem ginger, finely
   chopped, and 1 tablespoon of the
   syrup
1 egg white
1 tablespoon caster sugar
crystallized ginger, to decorate

Serves 6
Using an electric hand whisk, beat the yogurt, crème fraîche, lemon juice and zest and honey until light and fluffy. Add the chopped stem ginger and the syrup and beat again to mix in well.

In another bowl, with clean beaters, beat the egg white until it forms soft peaks. Add the caster sugar and beat again to form stiff, glossy peaks. Fold the egg white mixture into the yogurt and ginger mixture and spoon into 6 ramekins. Decorate with pieces of crystallized ginger, cover with clingfilm and freeze immediately for at least 6 hours, or ideally overnight, to set. Take them out of the freezer 10–15 minutes before you want to eat them.

Treacle Tart

My mum would occasionally buy a treacle tart as a treat – principally for my dad as a reward for doing hard graft in the garden. Dad loved treacle tart and I felt I should too, but they never seemed to live up to expectations. I found them to be always blandly sweet and gooey in a not-good way. But a homemade treacle tart is a different thing altogether. Lacing it with the tartness of citrus peel, juice and zest takes it beyond the realms of sticky and stodgy, to something worth many hours of digging and weeding. Penny provided the recipe for the pastry. I'm afraid, if it were up to me, I'd probably just buy a ready-made pastry case. Don't tell her, though.

FOR THE PASTRY
200g (7oz) plain flour, plus extra
  for dusting
125g (4½oz) butter
zest of ½ unwaxed orange
about 2 tablespoons cold water
salt

FOR THE FILLING
125g (4½oz) mixed candied peel
2 tablespoons lemon juice
260g (9½oz) golden syrup
zest and juice of 1 large unwaxed
  orange
175g (6oz) fresh brown or white
  breadcrumbs (or half of each)

Serves 6–8

Put the flour, butter, zest and a pinch of salt into a food processor and mix until it makes fine crumbs. Add just enough cold water to mix to a firm dough, wrap it in clingfilm and chill for 30 minutes. Soak the mixed peel in the lemon juice for 10–20 minutes.

Roll out the pastry on a floured work surface to a thickness of about 3mm (⅛in). Thin is good, as it makes the finished tart less heavy. If your pastry tears, just roll it back up into a ball and re-chill until firm before trying again. Line a loose-bottomed 20-cm (8-in) tart tin with the pastry and put it in the fridge. Any leftover pastry can be wrapped up well and frozen. Preheat the oven to 200°C (400°F), Gas Mark 6.

Heat the golden syrup, orange zest and juice in a saucepan until very runny, then stir in the breadcrumbs. Spread the soaked mixed peel over the pastry base, pour the warm breadcrumb mixture over the top and spread it out evenly. Bake for 10 minutes, then reduce the oven temperature to 180°C (350°F), Gas Mark 4, and bake for a further 25–30 minutes until the pastry is a light golden brown and the filling is set. Serve warm.

This freezes beautifully, just defrost and reheat before serving. Set the oven to 160°C (325°F), Gas Mark 3, cover losely with foil and reheat for 20–25 minutes or until warmed through.

SPRING TEATIME

Tea is, arguably, my desert island drink. Much as I love gin, cider or a cool glass of pink wine when the weather demands it, nothing, really, beats a mug of tea. Perfect on its own, but come that mid-afternoon energy slump, something treaty alongside that mug of tea can be just what's needed…

Welsh Cakes

I had never had a Welsh cake until I moved to Wales. I'm not sure really how best to describe them. They look a bit like flat scones, but are not as bready as a scone and (mercifully, in my mind) are not traditionally served with jam and cream. But neither are they really cakes. What they are is delicious, especially warm, straight out of the pan.

This recipe was written for Esse, the company that makes the cooker I use and the ones at River Cottage, by the wonderful Tim Maddams. He gave the traditional recipe a spicy twist which, although I was sceptical, works a treat.

110g (3¾oz) butter, cubed, plus extra for cooking
210g (7½oz) self-raising flour, plus extra for dusting
75g (2¾oz) golden caster sugar, plus extra for dusting (optional)

1 egg
zest of 1 small unwaxed orange or clementine
¼ teaspoon ground cardamom
75g (2¾oz) sultanas
cold milk (optional)

Makes 12–16

In a large bowl, rub the butter and flour together with your fingertips until you have a mixture that looks like breadcrumbs. Add the sugar, egg, orange zest, ground cardamom and sultanas. Mix with your hands to form a firm dough. If it is a little bit too dry, add a splash of cold milk.

Place the dough onto a floured surface, roll out until it is about 1cm (½in) thick and cut into rounds with a pastry cutter. If your cooker has a hot plate, you can cook these straight on that. If not, heat a heavy frying pan, melt in a bit of butter and then wipe it away with kitchen paper. Cook the Welsh cakes in the pan for 2–3 minutes until they are dark golden brown underneath, then flip and cook the other side. Serve warm just as they are, dusted with a little caster sugar, if you like, or serve them with butter, or – Tim's way – with a bit of goats' cheese and honey.

Polenta Cake
with Lemon & Pine

This was an experiment inspired, once again, by Liz Knight's quest to introduce the pleasure of wild, freshly gathered and free ingredients to everyday recipes. I had no idea that pine needles were edible, and although you wouldn't want to eat them by the handful, if used like a herb – as a substitute for rosemary, for example – they give a dish a soft, distinctive flavour which works really well with both savoury and sweet ingredients. This cake would normally use rosemary but I tried it with pine and added a scattering of pine sugar on the top, which although a rather surprising, unnatural-looking green, gives another layer of piney loveliness to this very easy-to-make cake.

200g (7oz) butter, softened

200g (7oz) caster sugar

3 large eggs

zest of 2 unwaxed lemons, juice of 1

2 teaspoons finely chopped light
  green pine needles, or rosemary

175g (6oz) ground almonds

1 teaspoon baking powder

150g (5½oz) fine polenta

2 tablespoons pine nuts

FOR THE TOPPING

2 tablespoons caster sugar

1 tablespoon pine needles

Makes 1 loaf

Preheat the oven to 170°C (325°F), Gas Mark 3, and line a 900-g (2-lb) loaf tin. Beat together the butter and sugar until light and fluffy. Then add the eggs, one by one, beating in between. Add the lemon zest and juice and the pine needles, then stir in the ground almonds, baking powder and polenta. Be careful not to overmix, but make sure all the ingredients are evenly distributed.

Spoon the batter into the prepared loaf tin, smoothing down the top. Scatter over the pine nuts and push them slightly into the batter. Bake for 50–60 minutes, or until a skewer inserted into the middle comes out clean. Loosely cover with a little foil or baking paper if the top is getting too dark during cooking. Once cooked, leave to cool in the tin on a wire rack until just warm. Then remove from the tin and leave on the rack until cooled completely.

Meanwhile, blitz the topping ingredients in a spice grinder (or well-washed coffee grinder) until you have a green sugar sprinkle. If you don't have a spice grinder, very finely chop the needles and bash in a pestle and mortar with the sugar until green and powdery. Sprinkle the top of the cake with the pine sugar topping before slicing. Alternatively, you can sprinkle it over the cake while still warm to give it a sugar crust.

SOME SPRING EXTRAS

A few little ideas to have stored away for later….

Pooch's Garlic

This is not something you can only do in spring, but it is so useful that it merited an early appearance in the book. Pooch is someone I think of as A Proper Cook. She knows how to correct things when they go wrong, what works as a substitute if you haven't got the right ingredients, what to do with a spider (not the eight-legged variety). And she is a veritable mine of Brilliant Things to Have In Your Fridge. This is one of them.

2–3 heads of garlic
olive oil

Makes about 20 cloves
Preheat your oven to 180°C (350°F), Gas Mark 4, or, if you are cooking something else at any temperature, you can cook these at the same time. Just adjust the cooking time accordingly.

    Put the whole heads of garlic on a baking tray and pop them in the oven. Remove when soft and golden. This will take about 45 minutes. Once cool enough to handle, pop the cloves out of their papery skins and put into a small, clean Kilner jar. Top up with olive oil. They will keep in the fridge indefinitely and give you an instant supply of soft, roasted garlic whenever you need it.

Rhubarb Vodka

One evening at our friend Katherine's house, we were offered a beautiful pink drink which turned out to be as delicious as it was decorative. 'It's rhubarb vodka,' she told us, 'I've got jars of it!' And sure enough, an entire shelf in her pantry was taken up by large Kilner jars of rhubarb seeping its unique flavour and lovely colour into otherwise absolutely bog-standard vodka. 'You should make some,' she encouraged me. 'I know how much you love rhubarb and it couldn't be easier to make.' So I did, and now it has become something of an annual ritual.

600g (1lb 5oz) rhubarb
rind of 1 unwaxed orange,
    removed in strips with a
    vegetable peeler

200g (7oz) caster sugar
1 litre (1¾ pints) vodka

Makes 1 litre (1¾ pints)
Start by sterilizing 2 Kilner jars by running them through the hot cycle of the dishwasher, or washing them in warm soapy water then drying them in a low oven (see page 226). Slice the rhubarb into thin slices and divide between the Kilner jars, along with the sugar, orange rind and vodka. Seal and put in a dark place for 6–8 weeks (the longer you leave it, the stronger the flavour), turning or shaking it every now and then.

When it has had its time, strain the vodka through a fine sieve or a muslin cloth and store in a screw-top bottle. It is best appreciated very cold and served neat in shot glasses. But with tonic, with lots of clinking ice and perhaps a slice of orange in the glass, or a slice of ginger, it is also rather good.

Elderflower Cordial

You will have to wait until late spring to make this. Elderflowers bloom from late May until mid-June and their delicate and distinct flavour is synonymous with long, lazy days, lying on sun-warmed grass, listening to the hum of bees. The cordial is made with the flowerheads, which are best picked on a warm, sunny day when the buds are freshly opened. Give them a little shake to remove any insects and a brief dunk in cool, clean water and drain on a clean tea towel before using.

Use white or pink elderflowers, or a mixture of both. If you want pink cordial, use pink flowers! The flowers infuse in their liquid overnight, but the cordial will be ready to use immediately.

1.5kg (3lb 5oz) sugar

2 litres (3½ pints) water

2 large oranges

3 lemons

60g (2¼oz) citric acid

20–25 heads of elderflower

Makes about 3 litres (5 pints)
Put the sugar and water into a large pan. Bring to the boil, stirring until all the sugar has dissolved. Remove from the heat. Slice the oranges and lemons and place in a large plastic bucket or stainless steel bowl along with the citric acid. Add the elderflower heads, pour the warm sugar syrup over and stir well. Cover with a lid or tea towel and leave somewhere cool overnight.

Strain the syrup through muslin to remove all the bits, then pour into sterilized bottles (see page 226). Store somewhere cool, and in the fridge once opened. The citric acid will help it keep for 3–4 months in the fridge. Or it can be frozen in plastic containers. You can also freeze the flowerheads and add them to the hot syrup straight from the freezer.

SUMMER

After all the frantic activity of spring, summer is a quieter season; a time, as is so often described, of long and – occasionally! – lazy days. I love the light mornings, the joy of being up and walking through the countryside before anyone else is awake. But I miss the birdsong, which has all but disappeared now breeding season is over. The chicks have fledged and the adult birds hide away to moult and recuperate after the rigours of raising their broods. So the woods are quiet, deeply shaded by a dense canopy of dark green leaves. But the insects are busy: in the veg patch and the garden, butterflies flit and bees hum and buzz. This is honey season. There are wild strawberries in the hedgerows and the ones I've planted are ready to pick. The tomatoes are fruiting and there are salad leaves and herbs and sweet peas and nasturtiums.

The animals on the farm are all back out in the fields. The cows, eager to come into their big warm shed in the winter, are just as eager to go back out again once the ground has dried up, the grass is fresh and green, and the air has lost its chill. They have

had their calves now, usually without help, taking themselves off to a quiet, tucked-away corner of a field to discreetly give birth to their big-eyed, gangly-legged youngsters. The lambs that were born in the spring will be growing fast and will no longer be dependent on their mothers. They'll be weaned, sorted and some will be sold. And it's shearing time, when the ewes and rams are relieved of their heavy winter fleeces. Shearing is an art form, a dance, a beautiful thing to watch (although fiendishly difficult to do). I roll the fleeces and stuff them into the wool sacks, watching the sheep spring away from the shearing pen almost unrecognizable – clean and lithe and unburdened.

As summer unfurls, we keep an eye on the hay fields, full of flowers and insects and swooping swallows. There'll be a time when the grass is long enough, but still sweet, and when the forecast is dry for a few days, that every lane and hay field will rumble with the sound of tractors as all the farmers cut, turn, bale and gather the hay. You can go to the fanciest restaurant in the world, but I promise you after an afternoon of loading bales onto a trailer, when you are hot and dusty and happily exhausted, nothing beats a picnic sitting on the freshly cut grass, back against a hay bale. Dogs sprawled at your feet. The flowery scent of hay in your nostrils. The evening sun warm on your face and a cool bottle of cider in your hand. That, for me, is summer.

A Soda Bread for Summer
with Tomatoes & Basil

A quick and gloriously simple loaf that is full of summery flavours. Lovely eaten with salad – think a classic Caprese, with this bread to mop up the olive-oily juices – or with a thick smear of fresh goats' cheese, or just a generous hunk, unadorned, when the hunger pangs strike…

250g (9oz) plain flour, plus extra
   for dusting
250g (9oz) seeded flour
1 teaspoon bicarbonate of soda
1 teaspoon salt
1 teaspoon dried thyme

60g (2¼oz) sunblush tomatoes
leaves from 1 stem of basil
300ml (10½ fl oz) buttermilk, or
   150ml (5fl oz) milk mixed with
   150ml (5fl oz) natural yogurt
oil for greasing

Makes 1 loaf

Preheat the oven to 200°C (400°F), Gas Mark 6. Mix the flours, bicarb, salt and thyme in a bowl. Chop the tomatoes and basil and add them to the dry ingredients. Stir in the buttermilk or milk/yogurt mixture until you have a dough. Scoop out onto a floured surface and shape into a roughly circular loaf.

Put on a greased baking tray and cut a deep cross in the top. Bake for 40–45 minutes, checking before you remove it from the oven that the bottom sounds hollow when tapped. Cool on a wire rack.

BREAKFASTS FOR SUMMER

I wrote a list of my favourite summery breakfasts and realized that almost everything on it could easily morph into a brunch or lunch dish, or a light supper. All Day Breakfast, anyone?

Herb & Feta Omelette
with Tomatoes & Oil

I love the gentle ritual of making an omelette, particularly that small, triumphant moment of sliding it from pan to plate, allowing it to fold over itself, revealing its golden brown underside. I know. I should probably get out more; but small moments of satisfaction such as these can really set you up for the day. That said, triumph only comes with a properly nonstick frying pan…

There are no rules for herb choice – just what you like or have in your fridge, on your window sill or in your veg patch. Parsley, chervil, dill, fennel, coriander, basil, oregano, thyme – all good. If you have mint, I'd add it, because mint, eggs and tomatoes seem to love being together. Perhaps avoid rosemary, only because it can be a bit difficult to chew.

2 or 3 eggs (depending on how
   hungry you are)
a handful of fresh, mixed herbs
olive oil

50g (1¾oz) feta, crumbled
1 or 2 tomatoes, or a handful of
   cherry tomatoes, sliced
salt and pepper

Serves 1
Beat the eggs in a bowl. Chop the herbs and add to the eggs along with a good pinch of salt and a grinding of pepper. Heat a glug of oil in a small, nonstick frying

pan over a medium heat. Tip your herby eggs into the frying pan and, with a spatula, gently push the eggs around a bit so you get an even cook. Personally, I don't like my omelettes cooked solid, so I cook them for barely a minute, sprinkling on the crumbled feta as the omelette gets to that just-cooked point.

Tip the omelette – with a small flourish! – onto a plate and serve alongside your sliced tomatoes, which you've sprinkled with salt and adorned with a drizzle of olive oil. Or, if you happen to have some, a summery-scented herb oil, like the one below.

Summer in a Bottle

There are lots of recipes for infusing herbs in oil – usually using those lovely, oily aromatic herbs like rosemary and thyme – which once made will last for a good while. This oil is one to make in small quantities and use within a fortnight, but it is lovely on lots of things, as well as alongside eggs. Great as a component for salad dressing (just add fresh lemon juice and salt and pepper), drizzled over soups or poached chicken or salmon, or just to dip a hunk of bread into.

60g (2¼oz) or so (you don't need to be too exact here) soft green herbs

300ml (½ pint) good olive oil or rapeseed oil

Makes 300ml (½ pint)
Before you start, have a bowl of iced water at the ready. Bring a pan of water to the boil, plunge your herbs into the boiling water and watch them like a hawk. You don't want them to lose their colour – so be prepared to take them off the heat after 10–30 seconds. Drain and put them immediately into the iced water and leave them there for about 5 minutes.

Dry them thoroughly on kitchen paper or a tea towel, then put them in a blender with about one-third of your oil. Blitz until you have a thick, green purée then add the rest of the oil and blitz again briefly.

You now need to filter it, either through a piece of muslin or a coffee filter lining a sieve, separating the herby sludge from what will become a deeply emerald-coloured, flavourful oil. I'd do it overnight – then you have a treat waiting for you in the morning, just in time for your omelette...

Goats' Cheese on Toasted Sourdough
with Thyme, Honey & Walnuts

We have a dairy down the road that specializes in making very fresh goats' cheese – more of a curd than a cheese. It doesn't have the very strong flavour some goats' cheeses can have, but does have that characteristic tang which goes so beautifully with the other flavours in this dish. It is a very simple, down-to-earth sort of breakfast – a holiday in Greece on a plate.

2 or 4 slices of sourdough bread
125g (4½oz) soft goats' cheese
runny honey

6–8 walnut halves
leaves from 4 sprigs of thyme
salt and pepper

Serves 2

Toast the slices of sourdough. Divide the goats' cheese between the slices and spread on thickly. Season with salt and pepper. Drizzle over the honey and crumble the walnuts on top. Scatter with the thyme leaves and eat dreaming of blue skies and warm seas.

If you want this for lunch, add some peppery salad leaves – rocket, watercress, mustard leaves – dressed with a little walnut oil and lemon juice.

Pink Grapefruit

with Strawberries, Rose Petals & Mint

My mum ate lots of citrus fruit when she was pregnant. Lemons were her favourite, which she ate like the rest of us might eat an orange. There have been scientific studies that link people's food preferences with what their mothers ate when they were pregnant, and I do adore lemons, although I don't eat them whole and unadorned. But I do love grapefruit just as they are. Mixed, as they are here, with gently macerated strawberries (I think of it as a sort of strawberry salsa) you get a lovely combination of sweet and sour. And the colours are beautiful. You can't eat this and not feel cheerful.

200g (7oz) strawberries
½ teaspoon rose water
2 teaspoons caster sugar
a few fresh rose petals

leaves from 2 stems of mint,
  finely chopped
2 pink grapefruit

Serves 2

Cut the strawberries into small pieces – quarters or eighths, depending on their size. Sprinkle with the rose water and sugar, a generous pinch of rose petals and half the mint and leave to macerate, if you can, for about 30 minutes. Peel the grapefruit, making sure you remove all the pith, then slice into thin rounds. Arrange the grapefruit slices on a plate and top with the strawberries, scattering them with the remaining mint and a few more rose petals.

This would also make a rather lovely, light pudding, perhaps served with a strawberry sorbet or (less light, but nonetheless worth considering) a very dark chocolate mousse.

A Breakfast Classic

The combination of smoked salmon and scrambled eggs is so well established as a breakfast classic, it has become something of a cliché. And often a disappointing one. There is nothing luxurious about a breakfast of overcooked eggs, served with greasy salmon on a tasteless bagel. Even more criminal is if the salmon is mixed in with the eggs.

This version is inspired by and in honour of my lovely friends Jonathan and Jo – AKA The Smokies. For the last 25 years, they have been running The Black Mountain Smokery and even Ludo's dad, who lived in Scotland and thought no one could smoke salmon properly south of the border, conceded that their smoked salmon was the best he'd ever tasted.

This breakfast is built around a fillet of hot-smoked salmon, which you can buy ready-prepared, but is also easy to do yourself. Jonathan showed me how, using just my little domestic barbecue. It takes a little bit of thinking ahead, but once done, it will keep for 3–4 days in the fridge and of course can be eaten in a myriad of ways for any meal you like.

Hot-smoked Salmon Fillets

I'm suggesting you do four fillets at a time, so you have a couple of extras to use for other things. You will need a barbecue with a lid and some woodchips – oak, maple or apple wood all work well. You can buy woodchips for smoking online or, if you have a local carpenter, like The Smokies do, ask if you can raid their woodchip pile. You are going to cure the salmon before smoking – so the whole process takes about four hours.

4 skin-on salmon fillets of equal
    size (about 150g/5½oz each)

2 tablespoons soft brown sugar
50g (1¾oz) fine sea salt

Makes 4 fillets

Lay the salmon fillets in a dish. Mix the sugar and salt together and cover the fillets with it. Put them in the fridge and leave for about 10 minutes. Then take them out, rinse the cure off, pat dry and return to the fridge for about 3 hours.

When ready, light your barbecue using a good handful of woodchips, then put the lid on to build up the heat and smoke. Once the woodchips are smouldering, put your fillets on a rack over the smoke, replace the lid of the barbecue and leave for 20 minutes, or until the fillets have turned opaque and are firm to the touch. Remove the fillets and allow to cool.

Hot-smoked Salmon
with Scrambled Eggs

a generous knob of butter
4 eggs
a few chives, snipped, plus extra to
    garnish

2 hot-smoked salmon fillets
salt and pepper
wedges of lemon, to serve

Serves 2

Melt the butter in a pan over a medium heat. Whisk the eggs and season with salt and pepper. Once the butter has melted, stir in the eggs and the chives and scramble until you get to the consistency you like (in my case, not too cooked – I like them to have that yellow gloss, not that dried-out look). Divide the eggs between 2 plates, alongside the salmon fillets. Sprinkle some extra chives over both eggs and salmon, and serve with lemon wedges on the side.

MAIN COURSES FOR SUMMER

✦

If the opportunity arises to eat outside, I always will. Eating in the open air makes me feel like I'm on holiday, even if I'm not. All the recipes that follow could happily be eaten outside and many of them could be cooked outside too.

Courgette, Lemon & Chilli Risotto

Marrow soup

Griddled courgettes

If you have ever grown courgettes, you will know that if you turn your back for too long, you end up with a bed of large, unwieldy marrows. One year, I chopped one up, put it in a pan with just a splash of water and let it cook until it was soft. It released so much water that when I blitzed it, it was the perfect consistency for a velvety soup. I added lemon zest and juice, a pinch of salt, and garnished it with red chilli and a drizzle of chilli oil. It was – I was delighted to discover – delicious. But then courgettes, lemon and chilli do complement each other in all sorts of guises. Here's another: griddle slices of courgette and dress with good olive oil and lemon juice, some salt and pepper, and top with finely sliced red chilli, lemon zest, torn basil leaves and toasted pine nuts. So it struck me that those flavours would work with the creamy nuttiness of arborio rice.

1 litre (1¾ pints) good vegetable
   stock (fresh or from a cube)
olive oil
50g (1¾oz) butter
1 small onion, finely chopped
1–2 red chillies, seeds removed,
   finely chopped
175g (6oz) arborio rice

a generous glass of white wine
1 large or 2 small courgettes,
   coarsely grated
zest of 1 lemon, juice of ½
50g (1¾oz) Parmesan, grated
1 tablespoon pine nuts, toasted
salt and pepper
a few basil leaves, to garnish

Serves 2

Begin by putting your stock in a saucepan, bring it to the boil and keep it gently simmering away with a lid on until you need it. Hot stock is, according to Those That Know, the key to a successful risotto. If you're using homemade stock, you might want to add some salt to it, to help with seasoning as you cook.

Heat a glug of oil and half the butter in a large saucepan or sauté pan, add the onion with a pinch of salt and let it sweat down, but don't let it brown. When it is translucent, add most of the chopped chilli, reserving some for the end. Stir the chilli around for a minute or so, then add the rice. Stir for a good couple of minutes to get warm and to be well mixed with the buttery onion and chilli.

Pour in the white wine. It should bubble as soon as it hits the pan. When it has been absorbed, add the hot stock, a ladle at a time, waiting for it to be absorbed between each ladleful, stirring all the while until the rice is just cooked, but still has bite (you may not need all of the stock).

Stir in the grated courgette with the lemon zest and juice. Stir to warm through and remove from the heat. Add the remaining butter and most of the Parmesan and stir vigorously so you get that beautiful creamy texture, flecked with the green of the courgettes, red of the chilli and yellow of the zest. Check for seasoning and add pepper and perhaps a bit more salt. Scoop into two warm bowls and garnish with toasted pine nuts, torn basil leaves and the remaining chilli and Parmesan.

A simple fresh, crunchy salad of sliced fennel and rocket with olive oil and lemon juice is what I love alongside this. And a glass of chilled pink wine. And the long, warm rays of the evening sun.

A Tray of Pizza
to Share

I've always felt mildly panicked at the thought of making pizza. I blame my lurking fear of dough and kneading and all those things. But this is a great, stress-free way of making pizza for a gang without any fancy equipment. Better still, because you are making one big tray of pizza, no one has to wait for their pizza to be ready while everyone else is tucking into theirs. And although it might not win prizes in Naples for authenticity, it is still that winning combination of a pungently sweet tomato sauce, cheese and luscious toppings on a thin, tasty dough. That needs no kneading. Need I say more?! It does, however, need at least three hours to rise, so don't think you can whizz this up for an instant supper. You might need takeaway for that.

Top tip here – use cooking (*cucina*) mozzarella rather than the fresh balls that are stored in water as they can make your pizza soggy. It is also worth investing in good-quality tomatoes for the sauce, such as San Marzano or any with a DOP label.

FOR THE DOUGH

500g (1lb 2oz) strong white bread
  flour
1 tablespoon fine sea salt
7g (¼oz) fast-action dried yeast
5 tablespoons olive oil
330ml (11fl oz) warm water

FOR THE TOMATO SAUCE

400g (14oz) can good-quality
  tomatoes
1 garlic clove, grated or minced
2 tablespoons extra virgin olive oil
4 basil leaves, finely torn
salt and pepper

FOR THE TOPPINGS

300g (10½oz) mozzarella, sliced

a selection of toppings, such as:

   chargrilled artichokes

   roasted red peppers

semi-dried tomatoes

roasted garlic

herbs

rocket

Serves 4

In a large bowl, mix the flour, salt and yeast until everything is evenly distributed. Add 2 tablespoons of the olive oil and the warm water and mix together really well until you have a smooth ball of dough. It is a bit of a sticky and messy process, but it will all come together. Or you can do it in a food processor if you have one.

Once your dough is ready, pour 3 tablespoons of the olive oil onto your largest baking tray (ideally around 45x30cm/18x12in) and spread it over the entire tray using your hands. Put the ball of dough onto the tray and roll it in the oil to coat. Squash and stretch the dough into a small, roughly rectangular shape, similar to that of your tray. It won't stretch to the edges at this point. You're just after a shape that is similar to your tray, but smaller. Cover loosely with oiled clingfilm and leave in a warmish place to rise for at least 3 hours or up to 12 hours.

Meanwhile, make the tomato sauce. Pour the can of tomatoes into a bowl and add the garlic, olive oil, ½ teaspoon of salt and the basil leaves. Using your hands, squash the tomatoes until finely pulped. You can use a stick blender if you prefer, but a bit of texture here is quite nice, so doing it by hand is best. Taste and adjust the seasoning if needed. You will have more sauce than you need, but it freezes really well and defrosts quickly, so you'll have a handy supply for your next pizza, or you can use it for a quick pasta supper.

Once your proving time is up, and the dough has risen to at least double its size and is spreading out on the tray, preheat your oven to its highest setting. Place a shelf on one of the bottom rungs of the oven.

Gently stretch the dough to the edges of the tray. Try not to knock out too much of the air. Leave it somewhere warm while you assemble all your toppings, so once you come to make your pizza you can do it as speedily as possible.

Once ready, spread a thin layer of the tomato sauce onto the dough, leaving a clean rim around the edge which will be the crust. Top with the slices of mozzarella and anything else you like (although please resist the urge for pineapple). Then put in the oven for 10 minutes. Check it at this point to see if your pizza base has turned golden. If it hasn't, give it a few more minutes. Remove from the oven and slide onto a wooden board for everyone to help themselves. No knives or forks needed, but napkins, or possibly bibs, are advised!

Mussels (& Cockles)
Cooked in Beer

I love mussels. I remember being slightly terrified of eating them because they look, well, just a bit wrong. But my dad, who adored shellfish, persuaded me to try them. I was instantly hooked on their lovely, soft-flavoured creaminess (unlike oysters, which I simply don't understand). If ever I see fresh mussels for sale either on a fish stall or in a restaurant, I buy them. Not least, because eating them transports me to one of my happy places. It is a restaurant – well, more of a large shack, actually – on the north coast of Brittany. We discovered it by chance while walking along the coast path one evening. It is called Le Crapaud Rouge – The Red Toad. It serves nothing but *moules frites*, which you eat with your fingers, washed down with a carafe of simple wine, sitting at a picnic table covered in a plastic cloth perched on the cliff above the sea. It is heaven. And you have to fight for a table.

The recipe opposite is inspired by two local friends – Ed, of Kingstone Brewery (which is, conveniently, just at the bottom of our hill), and Fabulous

Sarah, who runs the fish stall at our local farm shop. The classic way to cook mussels is in wine. I've also tried cider (excellent too). But it seemed mad, with a brewery right on the doorstep, not to try them cooked in beer. I asked Sarah what she thought and she couldn't believe I hadn't tried it before. 'It's fabulous!' she said, 'and if I can get you some cockles, chuck those in as well.' So I did.

1kg (2lb 4oz) mussels in their shells, or a mixture of mussels and cockles
oil
1 banana shallot, finely chopped
2 garlic cloves, sliced
1 long red chilli, finely sliced into rings (leave the seeds if you like the added kick)
2 lemongrass stalks, tough outer leaves removed, stems bashed

250ml (9fl oz) pale ale (I used Ed's Kingstone Gold)
100ml (3½fl oz) coconut milk or cream
Thai fish sauce
a small bunch of fresh coriander, torn
lime juice
sea salt flakes

Serves 2

Put your mussels in bowl of cold water, or the sink, and wash them. Throw out any that are slightly open and don't close when you tap them. Most mussels you buy now have been debearded, but if they still have fibrous, whiskery beards, just pull those off. Give the mussels a good rinse to get rid of any grit or sand.

Put a large pan or casserole with a lid over a medium heat, add a glug of oil and when it's hot, add the shallot, garlic, chilli and bashed lemongrass stalks with a pinch of salt. Fry, stirring so the onions don't burn, until the onions are soft and the lovely fragrance of chilli, garlic and lemongrass starts to tickle your nose.

Add the shellfish to the pan and pour over the beer. Bring to the boil, put the lid on and, every now and then, shake the pan. The shells will start to open. Keep the pan on the heat until they have all opened – which will take 3–4 minutes.

Keeping the pan on the heat, pour over the coconut milk or cream, add a few shakes of fish sauce, stir and then remove from the heat. Taste to see if it needs more fish sauce, then sprinkle with coriander and squeezes of lime juice. You can, if you are more refined than me, transfer the shellfish and their fragrant, beery juices to separate bowls (discarding any shells that haven't opened), or you can stick the pan between you and eat straight from it, with a large bowl for the empty shells and spoons and hunks of bread – Beer Bread even (see page 38) – for the juices. Oh, and kitchen roll. It's a gloriously messy business.

A FEAST FOR A SUMMER GATHERING

When I am President of the World, I will, along with banning plastic shower curtains and those horrible teacups you get in hotels, forbid the Breakfast Buffet. There is nothing pleasant about starting a day shuffling around with lots of other people poking at dishes of congealed eggs, scooping bits of tired-looking melon into a bowl or queuing to put a stale bagel into one of those useless toasting machines. In fact, there is no time of day that a buffet is okay.

And yet, as I write this, I can't quite see how the spread of recipes I'm about to suggest doesn't constitute exactly that: food that can all be made in advance, laid out in big dishes for people to help themselves. But not crowds of people, and perhaps that's the difference. This is a feast for about eight – although it is all food that can stretch to accommodate any last minute 'would you mind if I bring my kids/mother/girlfriend/dog.' And there are enough robust vegetable dishes for this to feed even the hungriest vegetarian, but with a poached chicken to keep the committed carnivores happy.

Lentil Salad
with Tenderstem Broccoli & Cherry Tomatoes

2 x 250g (9oz) packets of cooked
  Puy lentils, or 250g (9oz) dried
  Puy lentils, cooked and cooled
a bunch of flat leaf parsley, chopped
a bunch of basil, chopped
300g (10½oz) Tenderstem
  broccoli, steamed and refreshed
  in cold water

300g (10½oz) cherry tomatoes
  (mixed colours if you can get
  them), halved
juice of 1 lemon
olive oil
salt and pepper

Serves 8, as part of a feast
Put the cooked lentils in a large bowl along with the chopped herbs (reserving some to scatter over the top) and stir so the herbs are evenly distributed throughout the lentils. Add the broccoli and tomatoes, squeeze over the lemon juice, add a glug of olive oil and season well. Mix gently to combine and tip into a serving bowl. Scatter over the remaining herbs.

Roasted Peppers
with Mozzarella, Herbs & Capers

8 peppers (a mix of colours)
4 garlic cloves, finely chopped
a few sprigs of rosemary and thyme
olive oil
2 balls of mozzarella, drained
100g (3½oz) drained capers

a generous bunch of mixed green
  herbs (mint, basil, parsley,
  coriander, oregano, chives),
  chopped
50g (1¾oz) pine nuts, toasted
salt and pepper

Serves 8, as part of a feast
Preheat your oven to 200°C (400°F), Gas Mark 6. Halve and deseed the peppers and lie them on their backs in a large roasting tin. Scatter the garlic into the peppers along with the sprigs of rosemary and thyme. Keep these sprigs large as you will remove them when the peppers are cooked. Drizzle over olive oil and season with salt and pepper. Put them in the oven and roast for about 40 minutes until they are soft and slightly charred at the edges. Remove and let them cool in the tin.

When you are ready to serve, remove the sprigs of rosemary and thyme and transfer the peppers to a serving dish. Pour over the lovely, garlicky juices that will be left in the pan. Tear up the mozzarella and scatter over the peppers, along with the capers and your chopped mixed herbs. Sprinkle the pine nuts over the top.

Roasted Aubergines
with Roasted Garlic Yogurt & Pesto

I'm thinking half an aubergine per person here is enough, but do one each if you think I'm being mean. If you can get purple basil, it would look very pretty!

4 aubergines, halved lengthways	2–3 tablespoons pesto
olive oil	juice of ½ lemon
1 head of garlic	small handful of basil leaves, torn
300ml (½ pint) natural yogurt	salt and pepper

Serves 8, as part of a feast
Preheat your oven to 200°C (400°F), Gas Mark 6. Make a criss-cross of cuts in the flesh of each aubergine half and lay them skin side down in a roasting tin.

Brush with olive oil, pushing the bristles of the brush down into the cuts in the flesh. Season with salt and pepper. Tuck the head of garlic, just as it is, alongside the aubergines and roast for 50 minutes or so, until the aubergines are soft and browned. Remove from the oven and allow to cool in the pan.

Squeeze the cloves of garlic out of the skin and mash them in a bowl with a little salt. Add the yogurt, season with pepper and stir so everything is well mixed. Put the pesto in a bowl and thin it with the lemon juice so it is more like a thick dressing than a paste. Transfer the cooked aubergines to a serving dish. Top each half with a good blob of garlicky yogurt, and then drizzle the yogurt with pesto. Scatter the dish with torn basil leaves.

A Bowl of Proper, Old-fashioned Floppy Lettuce
With Dressing on the Side

I love these unpretentious summer lettuces with their soft, sweet-tasting leaves.

2 heads of round lettuce

2 teaspoons Dijon mustard

4 tablespoons white wine vinegar

8 tablespoons olive oil

pinch of sugar

salt and pepper

Serves 8, as part of a feast

Remove any tatty and discoloured outer leaves from the lettuces, then pull the rest gently apart from each other and plunge in a sink of cold water to rinse. Dry thoroughly and pile into a big wooden bowl.

Mix the mustard, vinegar and oil together, add a pinch of sugar and season. Put in a jug alongside the lettuce.

Poached Chicken
with Pangrattato & Tzatziki

Pangrattato is Italian for 'grated bread' – essentially breadcrumbs. But the Italian twist turns something that you might feed to the ducks into a crunchy, flavoursome addition to almost anything you can think of. Being the heathen that I am, I only discovered pangrattato recently. The base – breadcrumbs and garlic fried until crisp in olive oil – can be stored in a jar once cool for whenever you want a bit of crunch on pasta, a soup, a stew. And you can flavour it with different herbs, or chilli, or lemon zest, depending on your dish. It is also known as poor man's Parmesan, but that does something so delicious and adaptable an injustice.

FOR THE CHICKEN

1 large chicken, 1.8kg (4lb) or so	1 bay leaf
1 onion	1 teaspoon peppercorns
1 carrot	watercress, to serve

Serves 8, as part of a feast

Put the chicken in the biggest pot or saucepan you have. Cut the onion and carrot in half – no need to peel them – and put in the pot too, with the bay leaf and peppercorns. Place on the hob and pour in enough water to cover the chicken. Put the lid on, bring to the boil, then simmer until the chicken is cooked – about an hour. When the legs are wobbly and would be easy to detach from the bird, it's done.

Remove the chicken from the liquid and let it cool. The poaching liquid is now a rather lovely, easily acquired chicken stock, so worth keeping: you can boil it down a bit to reduce if you want, or just strain it. Let it cool and store in a tub or a bag in your fridge for up to 3 days, or freeze it.

Chicken stock

When the chicken is cool, gently remove the flesh from the carcass – which is easily done with your fingers – and arrange on a serving dish with the watercress.

FOR THE PANGRATTATO

2 tablespoons olive oil

2 garlic cloves, finely chopped

4 slices of stale bread, crusts removed, broken up into breadcrumbs by hand or in a food processor

a handful of mixed herbs (parsley, mint, chervil), finely chopped

zest of 1 unwaxed lemon

chilli flakes

1 teaspoon salt

Heat the oil in a frying pan over a medium heat and when it's warm, add the garlic and fry for a minute or 2 until its wonderful scent starts to rise from the pan. Add the breadcrumbs and fry until golden brown and crisp – which will take about 5 minutes. Remove from the heat and tip onto kitchen paper to cool.

Once cool, tip the breadcrumbs into a bowl and mix in the chopped herbs, lemon zest and a generous pinch of chilli flakes.

FOR THE TZATZIKI

½ cucumber

300ml (½ pint) natural yogurt

1 garlic clove

a small bunch of mint

olive oil

salt and pepper

Cucumber water

Peel the cucumber and slice it in half down the middle so you can scoop out the seeds by running the tip of a teaspoon down its length. Discard the seeds (or infuse in jugs of water for a refreshing cucumber flavour) and chop the cucumber into small chunks. Put in a colander with a sprinkling of salt and set aside for 10–15 minutes.

In the meantime, put the yogurt in a bowl. Crush the garlic into the yogurt and finely chop the mint leaves, then add the mint to the bowl, saving a bit for garnish. Season with salt and pepper and then add your cucumber. Mix and transfer to a serving bowl, drizzle with a bit of olive oil and sprinkle with the remaining mint.

When you are ready to serve, scatter the pangrattato over the chicken and bring it to the table with the bowl of tzatziki on the side.

Arrange all the dishes together on the table. Now gather your friends together, fill your glasses and feast!

A Few More Main Courses

Tomatoes with Steak
& Wild Salsa Verde

There is nothing more unappetizing than an over-chilled, woolly-textured, tasteless tomato. But to pluck a sun-warmed, perfectly ripe tomato from its stem, taking a moment to inhale the heady scent of the leaves as you do so, and to eat it, there and then, is sublime. My grandfather was a great tomato grower – a skill that has not been passed down to me, although I refuse to give up. Just the smell of tomato leaves rubbed between my fingers transports me back to being seven or eight years old, walking through my grandfather's greenhouse in his rather gruff wake, holding a bowl into which he would place the ripe fruit we would have for lunch with bread and cheese.

I could eat tomatoes, just on their own, by the plateful, their sweetness enhanced with nothing more than flakes of sea salt. However, they do go beautifully with very simply cooked steak, and tomatoes and steak combine very satisfactorily with the sharp, green acidity of a salsa verde. This is one of those meals that tastes elaborate and feels like a real treat, yet is testimony to the fact that good ingredients need almost nothing doing to them. Consequently, you can rustle this up faster than a bowl of pasta.

The salsa verde can be made in advance and will keep in a jar in the fridge for a few days. It will still be delicious if you only use bought herbs, but inspired by my friend Liz Knight, an inveterate and enthusiastic forager, I have used a recipe she shared with me which includes some wild alternatives.

Steak is a treat, something worth going to a butcher for, rather than buying it in a supermarket. Ben, the butcher at our local farm shop, will always advocate ribeye or sirloin over fillet steak as these cuts have more fat and therefore more

flavour. But he is a big fan of flank of beef, or bavette steak as it is also known, and so am I. Buy it in one piece – 300g (10½oz) should be enough for two people – then slice it against the grain and divide it up when it is cooked.

FOR THE SALSA VERDE
50g (1¾oz) sorrel
25g (1oz) rocket or bittercress
25g (1oz) spinach or chickweed
25g (1oz) mint leaves
25g (1oz) parsley or ground elder
25g (1oz) spring onions
2 garlic cloves

40g (1½oz) drained capers
1 teaspoon salt
1 teaspoon sugar
3 teaspoons Dijon mustard
100ml (3½fl oz) olive oil
cider vinegar

Makes 200g (7oz)
Finely chop the herbs, spring onions, garlic and capers and put in a bowl. Add the salt, sugar and mustard and stir to combine. Pour in the olive oil and then add a tablespoon of vinegar, stir and taste, adding more vinegar until you get the balance between oil and vinegar that you like. Adjust the seasoning – adding more sugar or salt if necessary. You want it to be sharp and zingy, but not eye-wateringly so. Will keep in the fridge for up to 3 days, stored in a sealed jar.

FOR THE REST
250g (9oz) mixed tomatoes
olive oil

a handful of chives
2 steaks, 150–200g (5½–7oz) each

Serves 2
Slice your tomatoes and lay them out in a serving dish. Drizzle with olive oil, and snip over the chives. Season with salt and a little pepper.

Cook the steaks on a barbecue or in a grill pan on the hob. Get the pan really hot. Season the steaks really well (but don't use oil as you will just fill your kitchen with smoke) and put them in the hot pan or over the coals. Cook for 2–3 minutes each side – you want them to be charred on the outside but still pink and luscious inside. Leave them to rest for 5–10 minutes, then serve with the tomatoes and salsa verde and a really good glass of red wine.

Roast Lamb
with Garden Veg, Oregano & Feta

A roast can feel like a rather heavy, wintery prospect for a summer day, but a roast leg of lamb somehow always feels summery to me – whereas the shoulder is more suited for winter, I think. The lamb here, accompanied as it is with pickings from the veg patch, fragrant oregano and tangy feta, is the centrepiece for a plate of food that is full of sunny flavours and won't leave you with that feeling of sleepy-eyed lethargy that comes after a hefty meal.

FOR THE LAMB

1 leg of lamb, about 2kg (4lb 8oz)

2 garlic cloves, sliced

olive oil

a handful of rosemary and thyme sprigs

a generous glass of red wine

Serves 6

Preheat the oven to 200°C (400°F), Gas Mark 6. Make sure your lamb is at room temperature before you cook it, so take it out of the fridge 20 minutes or so beforehand. With a knife, make small, deep cuts all over the leg of lamb and push a slice of garlic into each one. Rub over some olive oil and season well with salt and pepper.

Put the rosemary and thyme sprigs in the bottom of a roasting tin and place the lamb on top. Put in the oven and cook for about 1 hour and 10 minutes if you want your lamb to be pink (it is so much nicer when it is) or for longer if you want it cooked through. Remove from the oven, put the lamb on a board and let it rest for 10 minutes or so before you carve it.

Remove the rosemary and thyme sprigs from the tin and put it over a high heat on the hob. Add the wine to the juices and let it bubble for a moment or two to form a thin but tasty gravy. Pour into a jug and keep warm.

FOR THE VEGETABLES

400g (14oz) broad beans in their pods, or 200g (7oz) frozen broad beans

300g (10½oz) French beans

100g (3½oz) peas (fresh or frozen)

leaves from 3 sprigs of oregano

zest of 1 lemon, juice of ½

olive oil

50g (1¾oz) feta

salt and pepper

Serves 6

Cook the broad beans (shelled, if fresh) in boiling water for about 2 minutes. Drain and tip them into a bowl of cold water. Slip off the skins to reveal the bright emerald green beneath. This is, I admit, a bit of a faff, and you don't have to do it, but they taste so, so much nicer without the skins. Set aside. Cook the peas briefly in boiling water, drain and set aside. Trim the tails off the French beans and steam or plunge into boiling water and cook until they are al dente. Drain and put in a bowl together with the broad beans and the peas.

Finely chop the oregano leaves and add all but a few (saved for garnish) to the vegetables. Add the lemon zest and then drizzle over a bit of olive oil to make the vegetables glossy, but not swimming in it. Squeeze over the lemon juice, season with salt and pepper and mix gently. Tip into a pretty serving bowl, crumble over the feta and scatter with the remaining oregano leaves. Carve the lamb, pour the gravy over the slices and serve the vegetables alongside.

Summer Burgers

A few years ago, a young couple called Jess and Jake contacted us to ask if we would consider renting out one of the barns on the farm as a café. We were sceptical – the farm is off the beaten track. We'd tried to run a café there before and just hadn't been able to make it work. But Jess and Jake believed their route to success would be to specialize in serving one thing extremely well. And so it proved. The Pig & Apple has built up a loyal following that continues to grow – testimony to Jess and Jake's vision, hard work and their truly delicious burgers.

Jess and Jake will always say a burger can only be as good as the ingredients used to make it. Mercifully, times have changed from when the only burger you could get was some indeterminate bit of ground-up meat, turned into a mean, dry patty and sandwiched inside a flabby, tasteless roll. Now they have become a celebration of good ingredients, combined with a bit of culinary imagination. Although clearly there is no right or wrong time of year to eat a burger, for me they are the ultimate, eat-in-your-fingers, outdoors, sitting-on-the-grass summer treat.

The recipes for burgers that follow are courtesy of Jess and Jake. They would serve them in buns, with a wonderful array of garnishes and sauces and their spectacular chips on the side. I quite like a burger bunless, but with lots of relishes and simple sides, so I've added some ideas for relishes that might go well with each burger, a simple slaw with adaptations and some suggestions for flavoured butter to go with corn on the cob. The burgers are pan-cooked in these recipes, but you can, of course, fire up the barbecue and cook them over coals.

The Beef Burger

Really good mince is important here, so if you have a local butcher, ask for chuck steak, minced twice (for the best texture). Jake's (now not so) Secret Simple Burger Seasoning will make more than you need but it will keep indefinitely.

A tip from Jake: get your mince out of the fridge 20 minutes before you want to cook it. Any leftover burger seasoning would be delicious sprinkled on fries.

600g (1lb 5oz) good beef mince
oil

FOR JAKE'S BURGER SEASONING

1 teaspoon dried mixed herbs   1 teaspoon paprika
1 teaspoon garlic powder   2 teaspoons salt

Serves 4, with leftover seasoning

Divide the mince into 4 even portions and roll into balls.

Mix together the seasoning ingredients in a bowl and put in a spice shaker if you have one. Or just sprinkle it from a spoon or with your fingers.

Heat a dash of oil in a frying pan over a high heat. When the oil is hot, season the tops of the balls of mince with the burger seasoning and press down gently with a potato masher to push the seasoning into the meat and flatten out the balls just a bit. Put the patties into the oil, seasoned side down, and cook for 5 minutes.

Season the top sides of the burgers and flip them over for another 5 minutes of cooking. If you like your burgers a little rarer, reduce the cooking time slightly. Jake advises resting the burgers for 2 minutes before eating as it makes them extra juicy.

FOR THE BURGER RELISH

1 tablespoon tomato ketchup

3 tablespoons mayonnaise

1 teaspoon French's American
   mustard

1–2 gherkins, grated

Mix together the ketchup, mayo and mustard, then add a grated gherkin or two.

FOR THE HORSERADISH RELISH

4 tablespoons mayonnaise

1 teaspoon hot horseradish sauce

a handful of chives (about
   15g/½oz), finely chopped

Mix the mayonnaise with the hot horseradish sauce, then stir in the chives.

The Turkey Burger

600g (1lb 5oz) turkey mince

4 spring onions, finely chopped

1 red chilli, finely chopped

1 thumb-sized piece of ginger,
   peeled and grated

2 garlic cloves, grated

3 tablespoons hoisin sauce

1 tablespoon soy sauce

oil

Serves 4

Mix all the ingredients (except the oil) together thoroughly until well combined. Divide into 4 portions, roll into balls and place in the fridge. When you are ready to cook, put a glug of oil in a large frying pan over a high heat and when it's hot, add the turkey, flattening the balls down with your hand to form thick patties. Cook for 6 minutes a side over a medium heat, flipping now and again, until cooked through.

FOR THE PICKLED RADISH & GINGER RELISH

2 tablespoons rice vinegar

1½ tablespoons caster sugar

6–8 radishes, finely sliced

1 tablespoon drained sushi ginger,
   chopped

1 tablespoon chopped chives or
   spring onion

salt

Mix the vinegar, sugar and a pinch of salt together in a bowl, stirring to dissolve as much of the sugar as possible. Add the radishes, mix and allow them to sit and pickle for 10–15 minutes, stirring now and again. They can be left overnight at this point.

When you are ready, drain off the liquid, combine the radishes with the sushi ginger and chives or spring onion and serve.

The Pork & Chorizo Burger

150g (5½oz) chorizo, casing
   removed and finely chopped

450g (1lb) pork mince

oil

salt and pepper

Serves 4

Mix the chorizo with the pork mince with your hands. Season it really well, then divide into 4 equal portions and roll them into balls. Chill in the fridge until ready to cook.

When you are ready, heat a dash of oil in a pan and when it's good and hot, put the pork and chorizo balls into the pan, pressing them down with your hand to form thick patties. Cook for 6 minutes a side over a medium heat.

FOR THE SWEET PEPPER RELISH

1 jar of roasted red peppers, drained | salt and pepper
a handful of parsley, finely chopped

Blitz the roasted peppers with a stick blender or in a food processor until broken up but not smooth. Put in a bowl and stir in the parsley. Season with salt and pepper. Any leftovers will keep in the fridge for at least a couple of days.

And to Accompany the Burgers...

If you want your burgers in buns, Jess and Jake are firm believers in using brioche buns with the Beef Burgers, and sourdough buns for the Pork & Chorizo and the Turkey Burgers. The key is to toast them, so they don't go soggy. Jake puts them cut side down in the dry frying pan before cooking the burgers, until they are golden brown. For me, you can't go wrong with slaw and corn on the cob.

Simple Slaw
with Additions

¼ red cabbage | 2 large carrots
¼ white cabbage | sea and pepper

Serves 4

Shred the cabbage and grate the carrot. Mix together in a bowl and season.

To go alongside the Beef Burger: add a handful of chopped chives and a dressing made from 3 tablespoons of mayonnaise mixed with a teaspoon of French's American mustard and 4 tablespoons of the pickle juice from a jar of gherkins. Double the amount of mayo if you like your slaw heavily dressed and creamy.

To go alongside the Pork & Chorizo Burger: add a generous handful of rocket leaves to the slaw mix and dress with a chimichurri dressing made by mixing a small handful of finely chopped parsley and fresh coriander with a finely chopped red chilli, a grated clove of garlic, half a small finely chopped red onion, 7 tablespoons of olive oil and 2 tablespoons of red wine vinegar. Season with salt and pepper.

To go alongside the Turkey Burger: add a good handful of fresh coriander leaves to your slaw along with an Asian-inspired dressing made by whisking together 4 tablespoons of toasted sesame oil, 1 tablespoon of rice vinegar, 1 tablespoon of soy sauce, 1 teaspoon of sugar and the juice of half a lime.

The Corn on the Cob

As someone who shamelessly admits to enjoying food far more if it is eaten without the burden of cutlery, corn on the cob is a perfect vegetable for me. I love its sweet crunch and the charred smokiness if its cooking has been finished off over fire. I don't even mind the bits getting stuck in my teeth. And it is wonderfully, finger-lickingly messy, particularly if it is slathered in butter, which is the law.

Butter for cobs to accompany the Beef Burger: Beat 50g (1¾oz) softened butter with 1 teaspoon of chipotle chilli flakes. Then chill.

Butter for cobs to accompany the Pork & Chorizo Burger: Beat 50g (1¾oz) softened butter with a handful of finely chopped parsley and a clove or two of grated garlic. Then chill.

Butter for cobs to accompany the Turkey Burger: Beat 50g (1¾oz) softened butter with a generous teaspoon of white miso. Then chill.

Gin-cured Salmon

with Rye Soda Bread, Dill Potato Salad & Pickled Cucumber

꘎

Nina and her husband Joe started the Silver Circle Distillery in an agricultural shed on the edge of our neighbouring village. Their flagship product is Wye Valley Gin, a beautiful blend of local botanicals, but they also distil small batches of seasonal gins and vodkas, using ingredients like local honey, pears, damsons and garlic. Much as I love drinking their gin, I had never thought to cook with it.

This recipe is Nina's, inspired by her Swedish roots, and it is an absolutely revelatory way of preparing salmon. Although it involves almost no work, the curing process takes 24–36 hours, so do plan ahead. It'll be worth it. In keeping with the Swedish-inspired theme, I have included a couple of ideas to go with it.

Gin-cured Salmon

Choose a piece of salmon cut from the centre of the fillet if possible. You want a piece that is roughly rectangular.

500g (1lb 2oz) piece of skin-on, salmon fillet

150g (5½oz) caster sugar

150g (5½oz) coarse sea salt

50ml (2fl oz) gin

40g (1½oz) dill

Serves 4

Put the salmon, skin side down, in a baking dish big enough so it can lie flat. Mix the sugar, salt and gin together in a bowl. Chop up the dill, including the stalks, and add it to the gin curing mixture. Stir it in, then spread the cure over the salmon, making sure all the flesh – including the sides – is covered in the lovely, green-flecked, salty, sugary, gin-soaked mixture.

Cover the salmon in a few layers of clingfilm, pressed down against the flesh, then put a board or a plate on top of it and weigh it down with a kitchen weight or a couple of cans or jars. Put it in the fridge to 'cook'. And it really does effectively cook. If you like a light cure, leave it for 24 hours. If you prefer it a bit more cured, leave it for 36 hours.

When it's had its time, take it out of the fridge and scrape off as much of the cure as you can. Don't worry about the dill, which will cling, it's the salt and sugar you need to remove. Give it a quick rinse under the cold tap and pat it dry with kitchen paper.

It is now ready to eat. I like it sliced as you would a loaf, each slice around 5mm (¼in) thick, or a bit less. The skin will just gently peel off. It is, I promise, soft and meltingly delicious.

Rye Soda Bread

Rye bread is a quintessential part of Scandinavian meals but making it from scratch is a time-consuming affair, and if you are an inexperienced bread maker like me, it feels like too many things could go wrong. However, our failsafe friend soda bread can be made with rye flour and, honestly, I think it is just as good.

25g (1oz) oats
25ml (1fl oz) boiling water
400ml (14fl oz) natural yogurt
1 tablespoon brown sugar

400g (14oz) wholemeal rye flour
  (Talgarth Mill do a great one)
1 teaspoon fine sea salt
1½ teaspoons bicarbonate of soda

Makes 1 loaf
Preheat your oven to 180°C (350°F), Gas Mark 4. Put the oats into a bowl with the boiling water and leave to soak for 10–15 minutes. Once they are nicely mushy, stir in the yogurt and sugar. Then mix in the flour, salt and bicarbonate of soda until everything is combined and you have a sticky dough. Scoop out onto a floured work surface and shape into a long baton. Put on a greased baking tray and cook for 45–55 minutes. Give its bottom a tap and if it sounds hollow, it's done. Cool on a wire rack.

New Potato Salad
with Dill

Potato salads made with lots of gloopy mayonnaise are pretty high on my list of Food I Never Want To Eat. But this has no mayonnaise, just a lovely, quietly zingy dressing that doesn't mask the delicate flavour of the new potatoes. And there is more dill. Dill overkill, you might think, but you'd be wrong!

1kg (2lb 4oz) new potatoes,
  scrubbed if they need it
20g (¾oz) dill
1½ teaspoons Dijon mustard
2 spring onions, finely sliced

150ml (¼ pint) olive oil
zest and juice of 1 unwaxed lemon
1–2 pinches of sugar
salt and pepper

Serves 4

Halve or quarter the large potatoes so they are all roughly the same size. Put them in a large pan of cold water with a couple of pinches of salt. Bring to the boil and cook until they are tender, but not collapsing. Drain and leave to cool.

Meanwhile, to make the dressing, cut the stalks off the dill and chop two-thirds of the leaves finely (the rest is for the garnish). Put the chopped dill leaves into a jug or small bowl with the mustard, spring onion and oil. Season with salt and pepper, add the zest and juice of the lemon and a pinch or two of sugar. Whisk everthing together, have a taste to see if it needs more sugar or salt, then pour over the potatoes. The potatoes can sit, dressed, quite happily in the fridge for a couple of days, or you can eat them straight away, sprinkled with the remaining dill.

Quick Pickled Cucumber

This quick pickled cucumber is lovely with lots of things, including the burgers on pages 121–5 or just alongside a hunk of cheese. Its perky, fresh, sharpness is also the perfect foil for the richness of the gin-cured salmon on page 128. I've included dill in the ingredients list here, which really might be overdoing it if you serve it alongside the salmon and the new potato salad above, but is a nice addition otherwise.

2 cucumbers

3 teaspoons salt

1 tablespoon fennel seeds or
    coriander seeds (optional)

1½ tablespoons white wine vinegar

1½ tablespoons caster sugar

a handful of chopped dill
    (optional)

Serves 4

Halve the cucumbers lengthways, scrape out the seeds with a teaspoon and slice the flesh finely. Put it in a bowl, sprinkle over the salt and massage it into the cucumber with your hands. Transfer to a colander, cover with a plate and weigh the plate down with a tin or jar of something. Leave the cucumbers to drain for about 20 minutes.

If you are adding the fennel or coriander seeds, gently toast them in a dry frying pan until fragrant, then set aside to cool.

Once the cucumbers have had their time, squeeze them between your hands to get rid of any excess water, then pat them dry. Mix the vinegar and sugar together in a bowl then add the cucumber. Toss together with the seeds and/or dill if you are using it and serve.

Brock Choc Chip

This is Freddie's favourite 'because it is very simple and very nice. If you like chocolate. And ice cream.' The beauty of making chocolate chip ice cream this way, rather than with actual chocolate chips, Freddie tells me – and I can confirm – is that you get finer shards of chocolate throughout the ice cream, giving it a lovely texture. And occasionally you strike gold and get a big lump of chocolate all to yourself...

FOR THE CUSTARD BASE

6 egg yolks (save the whites to make meringues

200g (7oz) caster sugar

3 tablespoons skimmed milk powder

1 litre (1¾ pints) whole milk

150ml (¼ pint) double cream

150g (5½oz) dark chocolate

100g (3½oz) white chocolate

Serves 8–10

Whisk the egg yolks, sugar and skimmed milk powder together until smooth and pale. Put the milk and the cream in a saucepan and heat until bubbles form at the side but it doesn't actually boil. Take the pan off the heat and pour it into the egg mixture. Have your pot-washer thoroughly clean the pan while you stir. Then pour the mixture back into the pan, return it to a gentle heat and warm until it reaches 75°C (167°F). Take it off the heat and let it cool. Once it has cooled, chill it in the fridge overnight.

The next day, bring out the custard base and start to churn it. In the meantime, melt the dark chocolate in a bowl over a pan of gently simmering water, and the white chocolate in another bowl. When the ice cream has started to solidify, gently trickle the dark chocolate into the mix as it churns. Then do the same with the white chocolate. When the ice cream has reached that lovely soft, frozen consistency, scoop it out into a tub and freeze it.

PUDDINGS FOR SUMMER

Frankly, if there are fresh strawberries to be had or a sun-warmed peach, I wouldn't bother with a pud, but then there are some puddings, so synonymous with the happy, warm contentment that accompanies a lazily sociable summer's day that it would be remiss of me not to include them.

Contrary Cheesecake

The contrariness here is all mine. I generally avoid cheesecake – but a deconstructed cheesecake is somehow okay. In fact, not just okay, but very delicious indeed. This recipe is a sort of mash-up of a cheesecake my mum makes and one that my friend Penny makes, but done my contrary way. It requires a little light beating to make the creamy bit and a bit of bashing to make the crunchy bit, and is very amenable to any adaptations and additions you might want to make. I've made a few suggestions on page 136.

FOR THE CREAMY BIT

250g (9oz) mascarpone
150g (5½oz) cream cheese (I use a light one because I prefer the texture, but full-fat is fine too)

25g (1oz) caster sugar
zest and juice of 1 unwaxed lemon
½ teaspoon vanilla extract
100ml (3½fl oz) double cream

Serves 4–6

With an electric hand whisk, beat together the mascarpone, cream cheese, sugar, lemon zest and juice, vanilla extract and cream until smooth and well combined. Chill in the fridge. You can chop and change your citrus flavours at will – use an orange, a lime or two, or a clementine – and play around with the biscuit base accordingly.

FOR THE CRUNCHY BIT

100g (3½oz) ginger nut biscuits (about 10)	30g (1oz) butter

Put the biscuits in a bowl, break them up a bit with your hands and then bash them a bit with a rolling pin until you have a nicely uneven crumb. Melt the butter in a saucepan, add the biscuit crumbs and stir so they are well coated. Pour the mixture into a nonstick tin (you are going to break this base up, remember, so it can be any size tin), pat the crumb down with a wooden spoon then put the tin in the fridge.

You can add 1 tablespoon of cocoa powder (or more) to the mix to make a chocolate ginger crumb. Or use digestive biscuits instead. I've added a handful of chopped hazelnuts on occasion too. Add a teaspoon of spice – cinnamon or mixed spice for a wintery version.

To serve

350g (12½oz) mixed summer berries	mint leaves (I like to chop them into ribbons)
zest of 1 unwaxed lime, plus a squeeze of juice	icing sugar

How you present this pud is really up to you. In glasses, a bowl or a plate. Biscuit crunch beneath the cream and the fruit, or on top. Anything goes. I like the berries mixed gently with the lime juice and zest, some of the mint leaves and just a sprinkling of icing sugar. I'd serve them alongside a generous blob of the lemony topping, scatter the ginger crunch with abandon and decorate with a couple more mint leaves.

When berries aren't in season, the Rhubarb Compote on page 232 will go well (perhaps with orange rather than lemon in the creamy bit). Or frozen fruit, like cherries or blackcurrants, gently thawed and served warm alongside it – in which case I might go against type and serve it in a glass to make the most of the juice.

Jellies

School food, if like me you grew up in the 70s, was not anything to look forward to. Instant mash potato, always cold, always with suspicious lumps in. Spam. Luncheon meat. Baked beans. Cubed pickled beetroot. But the highlight was pudding on a Friday which was always jelly (bright red in colour but with no discernible flavour) and ice cream. I hated both and so was immensely popular because I would share out my portion among the others on my table when our teacher wasn't looking.

For years and years the very thought of jelly made me go, well, a bit wobbly. Then recently – like in the last two or three years – I discovered the joy of jelly. Light, refreshing, perfect for a summer day and you can have endless fun experimenting. And – weirdly (but maybe that is genetics for you) – my mum, who also claimed she hated the stuff, discovered she loved it too. And makes it all the time now. So here are a couple of Humble favourites:

Rhubarb & Ginger Jelly

2–3 stalks of rhubarb, trimmed

zest of 1 unwaxed orange, juice of ½

runny honey or maple syrup

1 packet of orange jelly

ginger beer

ginger wine (optional)

Serves 4

Cut the rhubarb into chunks. The size will depend on what you want your final jelly to end up in – individual glasses or ramekins, or one big bowl. Put the chunks in a pan with the orange zest and juice and add runny honey or maple syrup to taste. Poach until the rhubarb is soft but still holds it shape – about 5 minutes. Arrange the rhubarb on the bottom of the dish of your choice and leave to cool.

Cut up the jelly and put it into a measuring jug. Dissolve it in a little boiling water, then top up with ginger beer until you have 500ml (18fl oz) of liquid. (Mum also advocates using a splash of ginger wine if you have it. I'm beginning to realize, as she sends me more of her recipes, that she advises putting booze in almost everything.)

Pour your jelly mixture over the rhubarb and leave to set in the fridge.

Elderflower Jellies

12g (⅜oz) powdered gelatine

5 tablespoons warm water

150ml (¼ pint) elderflower

    cordial (either shop-bought or

    homemade – see page 80)

350ml (12fl oz) cold water

a few elderflowers or other edible

    flowers

Serves 4

Sprinkle the gelatine over the warm water in a small saucepan. Stir well to dissolve. If the gelatine has not completely dissolved after a couple of minutes, then put over a low heat, stirring until the gelatine completely dissolves. Do not allow to boil. Leave to cool until no hotter than lukewarm.

In a jug, mix together the cordial and the cold water. Stir in the gelatine, mix well, then pour into 4 white wine glasses or tumblers, adding a few edible flowers as you pour, if you like, so they are spread throughout the elderflower jellies. Allow to set for 3–4 hours in the fridge. Remove from the fridge 10 minutes before serving and decorate with more flowers.

Raspberry Sorbet

with Poached Peaches or Nectarines

This is Penny's recipe and it is a truly beautiful sorbet – almost vermillion in colour and as vibrantly flavoured. And atop a gently poached peach or nectarine, it is nothing short of utopian.

Raspberry Sorbet

You can make this sorbet with or without an ice cream-maker, but if you do use a machine, leave out the gelatine. This is best eaten the day after you make it.

½ teaspoon powdered gelatine
  (optional – see above)
5 tablespoons warm water
  (optional)

375g (13oz) granulated sugar
375ml (13fl oz) boiling water
450g (1lb) raspberries
juice of 2 lemons

Makes 1 litre (1¾ pints)

If you are making this without an ice cream-maker, sprinkle the gelatine over the warm water in a small saucepan. Stir well to dissolve. If the gelatine has not completely dissolved after a couple of minutes, put over a low heat and stir until it does. Do not allow to boil. Leave to cool until no hotter than lukewarm.

Make a sugar syrup by putting the sugar in a jug, pouring over the boiling water and stirring until dissolved. Add the gelatine (if you are using it) and leave to cool. Once cool, put your raspberries and the sugar syrup in a blender and purée until smooth, then strain through a sieve to remove the pips. Stir in the lemon juice and chill in the fridge for a few hours or overnight.

If you are using an ice cream-maker, tip the raspberry mixture into the bowl and let it churn until frozen. If you are not using a machine, put the mixture in a tub and place in the freezer until it is mostly, but not completely, frozen – about 5–6 hours. Scoop it out into a blender and blitz it a bit to break it up, then put it back in the tub and freeze overnight. Remove the sorbet from the freezer 20 minutes before you want to eat it and put it in the fridge to soften.

Poached Peaches or Nectarines

2 peaches or nectarines, not too ripe	500ml (18fl oz) boiling water
125g (4½oz) sugar	1 star anise

Serves 4

Wash the fruit and split into halves. Using a sharp vegetable peeler, peel the skin off. Put the sugar and boiling water into a jug and stir to dissolve. Put the peach halves and star anise in a small pan, then pour over enough hot sugar syrup to cover them. Bring the syrup to a simmer, then turn off the heat and leave them to sit in the syrup as it cools. Serve either while still slightly warm, or chilled.

Summer Pudding

Our friend Felicity grew up just inland from Lyme Regis on the Dorset coast. For a few years, every summer a gang of us would descend on her ever-patient parents and spend a weekend, barefoot and carefree, hanging out in their beautiful garden. And we had a ritual which we rarely wavered from. On Saturday we would head into Lyme and go out on one of the small fishing boats with hooks and a line, hoping to catch enough mackerel to feed us. Then, on our way back to the house, we'd stop at the pick-your-own fruit farm and gather punnets of strawberries, raspberries and currants. Together we'd sit at the garden table to prepare the fruit, which would be piled into a bread-lined basin and left in the pantry, weighted down with a couple of cans of tomatoes.

On Sunday, we'd feast. The mackerel would be cooked over a fire, eaten with tomatoes and salad from the veg patch. The basin would be retrieved from the pantry and, with nerve-wracking ceremony, carefully upended onto a plate to reveal a dome of juice-soaked bread encasing the luscious fruit. Whenever I make or eat summer pudding now, it is with happy nostalgia for those heady days.

You will need a pudding basin about 15cm (6in) in diameter.

500g (1lb 2oz) summer berries, stalks removed, any large pieces halved

175g (6oz) caster sugar

400g (14oz) brioche, sliced

strawberries, to decorate

cream, to serve

FOR THE BLACKCURRANT COULIS

1 small punnet of blackcurrants, about 125g (4½oz)

2–3 tablespoons caster sugar

Serves 4

Begin by making a blackcurrant coulis. Put the blackcurrants into a pan with the sugar (to taste) and just a splash of water to stop them sticking to the bottom of the pan. Cook over a medium heat until the currants are soft – about 5 minutes. Push them through a sieve into a bowl. Discard the skins and pips and set aside the bowl of coulis.

Put the summer berries in a saucepan with the caster sugar and a tablespoon of water. Heat gently until the fruit has softened, but hasn't lost its shape. Tip the fruit into a sieve over the bowl of blackcurrant coulis to add the fruit juices to the coulis. Taste the coulis and add a little more sugar if needed.

Line the pudding bowl with clingfilm – a little moisture on the bowl will help it stick to the sides. Cut all the crusts off the brioche and roll each slice lightly with a rolling pin, so they end up about half the thickness. Cut one piece to cover the base of the pudding bowl.

Pour a bit of the fruit coulis onto a deep plate and dip your cut piece of brioche in it so that it is juice-soaked on one side. Lay it, juice side down, in the bottom of the basin. Then do the same with the slices of brioche, cutting to size and pressing them into the sides of the bowl until it is lined completely, with no gaps.

Fill the bread-lined basin with the fruit, pressing it gently down so it is packed in. Then top with more slices of dipped brioche – juice side up. Cover with clingfilm and a plate that fits just inside the bowl. Put a weight on top – a can of tomatoes or something – and leave in a cool place or the fridge for 24–48 hours. Keep the leftover coulis to serve with it when it is ready.

When you are going to eat it, turn it out onto a plate, remove the clingfilm, decorate with fresh strawberries and serve in generous slices with the remaining coulis and some cream poured over.

SUMMER TEATIME

Perfect treats for picnics or the summer fete.

Raw Chocolate Brownies

When brownies are good, they are very, very good, but when they are not they can be teeth-suckingly sweet and cloying or densely stodgy and dry. But in a café in a small town in mid-Wales – one of those comfortably shabby, lovely places full of books and newspapers and dogs and people wearing tie-dye – I discovered raw chocolate brownies. If you are a purist, this whole idea might be too out there to contemplate. But to me, they were a revelation. This is my version of them.

200g (7oz) pitted dates – Medjool
   are best as they are the squidgiest
100g (3½oz) skin-on almonds
60g (2¼oz) coconut oil
2 tablespoons maple syrup
40g (1½oz) dark cocoa powder
½ teaspoon sea salt flakes
25g (1oz) freeze-dried raspberries
75g (2¾oz) walnuts, coarsely
   chopped

FOR SPRINKLING ON TOP
icing sugar
freeze-dried raspberries, crushed
2 teaspoons dried rose petals
toasted flaked almonds

Makes 16–20

Line a square 20-cm (8-in) brownie tin (or other tin of a similar size) with baking paper. Put all the brownie ingredients, apart from the raspberries and walnuts, in a food processor. Blitz until everything is well mixed and you have a smooth, thick paste. The mixture may seem a bit firm, but bear in mind that this is it – you've just made your brownie. It is going to 'cook' in the fridge, so you don't want the mixture to be remotely sloppy. Transfer the mixture to a bowl and stir in the raspberries and roughly chopped walnuts, then scoop into your prepared tin and press it down. Chill in the fridge for at least 2 hours.

When ready to serve, remove from the tin. Dust with icing sugar and crushed dried raspberries and decorate with rose petals and toasted flaked almond. Cut into squares (a sharp knife dipped in a mug of boiling water will give you neat squares). Their richness is nicely counterbalanced with fresh berries and perhaps a spoon of coconut yogurt.

Honey Lemon Drizzle Cake

If there were a *Desert Island Discs* equivalent for cakes, it would be almost impossible to choose whether to save the lemon drizzle or the old-fashioned, booze-laden fruitcake from the incoming tide. Penny's lemon drizzle has made many a guest at the farm swoon, so it really didn't need tinkering with, but she was intrigued by my suggestion of adding some local honey to the mix. So we tried it. I think the bees would have been proud.

225g (8oz) butter, softened, plus
   extra for greasing
225g (8oz) granulated sugar
100g (3½oz) runny honey
275g (9¾oz) self-raising flour

2 teaspoons baking powder
4 large eggs
1 tablespoon milk
zest of 2 large unwaxed lemons,
   juice of 1

FOR THE DRIZZLE
juice of 1 lemon

70g (2½oz) runny honey
35g (1¼oz) caster sugar

Serves 10

Preheat the oven to 180°C (350°F), Gas Mark 4, and grease and line a roasting tin – about 30x20x5cm (12x8x2in) – with baking paper.

Put all the cake ingredients into a large bowl and beat with an electric hand whisk until well combined and smooth. Spoon it into the prepared tin and level the top.

Bake in the oven for 35–40 minutes, until the cake has shrunk from the sides of the tin and a skewer comes out clean from the centre. Leave to cool in the tin, on a wire rack.

While it cools, make the drizzle. Warm the lemon juice with the honey in a small pan. Pierce the surface of the cake with a fork, about a dozen times. Add the caster sugar to the warm mixture and spoon this gradually over the cake, giving it time to be absorbed between spoonfuls. Leave to soak in then, once completely cool, slice and serve. This will freeze in the unlikely event you have any left.

SOME SUMMER EXTRAS
୰

Two entirely contrasting ideas here: one floral and fragrant, the other fiery and nose-tingling and best kept for later.

Chilli Sherry

It was Ludo who introduced me to chilli sherry. He had grown up with an ever-present bottle of it in his family kitchen. His mother made it by poking a handful of chillies into a bottle, topping it up with sherry and letting it sit until the sherry had become infused with the warm heat and potency of the chillies. She would add it to soups and stews, transforming a slightly bland dish into something that has real depth of flavour and a gentle kick. Put a splash in a ragu, or a Bloody Mary, or mince for a shepherd's pie.

And once you've made your chilli sherry, you can keep topping up the bottle. Ludo is convinced his mother had the same bottle for years. The bottle in our kitchen has been on the go for at least a decade. It is one of the most useful ingredients I have. If you do make this in the summer, come winter, when it has had time to really infuse, I won't mind betting you'll be sloshing it into everything. But I have included a recipe on page 274 to start you off. You will need a 1-litre (1¾-pint) glass bottle with an airtight lid.

6–8 mixed chillies

1 bottle of dry sherry (Fino or similar)

700ml (1¼ pints)

Prick the chillies with the point of a knife. Any that are too fat to fit down the neck of the bottle, cut in half. Push them into the bottle and fill it with the sherry.

Let it sit, undisturbed, for 3–4 days. The heat will start to gradually seep into the sherry. The longer you keep it, the stronger it becomes but, as I say, you can just keep topping it up.

Summer in a Teapot

I'm a bit of a herbal tea junky, as my kitchen cupboard will testify. Even if I have several boxes on the go, I find myself wooed all too easily by enticing packaging and flavour combinations. And I'm not alone, it seems. Industry research expects the global herbal tea market to be worth well over a billion US dollars in the next five years.

But come summer, you can make your own unique and bespoke herbal teas from plants that you might have growing in your garden or on your window sill. Mint (see page 33) is an obvious example, but lemon verbena, lavender, rosemary, camomile – all ingredients that crop up in many of the shop-bought herbal tea mixes – can very easily be grown at home, picked fresh and infused in hot water to create an aromatic, healthy brew. One of those teapots that has a built-in strainer is ideal. Here's one idea for a combination of herbs that makes, what I think of, as summer in a tea pot.

2 sprigs of rosemary

2 sprigs of lemon thyme

1 flowerhead of fennel

2 stalks of lavender with flowers

300ml (10fl oz) freshly boiled
   water

Serves 2

Put all the herbs in a tea pot. Pour over the freshly boiled water and let infuse for 5 minutes before drinking.

AUTUMN

If I were pushed to choose a favourite season, I think it would be autumn. It is a time of such dynamism, of change and colour and extraordinary beauty. Misty mornings, dewdrops on spiders' webs, wild storms and whirling leaves, mellow golden sunshine, a nip and freshness to the air. There are apples, plums and pears in the garden, blackberries and rosehips in the hedgerows, cobnuts and acorns and beech mast and mushrooms.

On the farm, the summer hay crop is stacked up in the sheds, the cattle barns are made ready for when the cows come in for the winter, hedges are laid. As the days shorten the ewes and female goats come into season. Put the most handsome, virile ram or billy goat in with them in July and they won't show the slightest interest, but as the nights draw in, the idea of a woolly liaison is rather more appealing. The rams – or tups as they are also known – are checked and given extra feed so they are in peak condition for the job and the calendar is consulted. The gestation period for sheep and goats is five months. We want some lambs in February

and some in late March, so the rams will be put in with half the ewes in mid-September and the others a month or so later.

This is cider-making season, a time for chutneys and stews and crumbles. For foraging alongside the busy squirrels and jays, accompanied by the roar of the stags who are establishing territories and gathering their harem of females. For the comfort of jumpers and thick socks and bobble hats. For the fire to be lit and the smell of mulling spices, warm bread and soul food to come from the kitchen.

A Soda Bread for Autumn
with Red Peppers

I love goulash, that heart-warming Hungarian staple. This bread is a homage to the rich warmth that comes from soft, roasted peppers and the gentle, smoky intensity of paprika.

250g (9oz) spelt and rye flour
  mixed
250g (9oz) wholemeal flour
1 teaspoon salt
1 teaspoon bicarbonate of soda
2 teaspoons smoked paprika

100g (3½oz) drained roasted
  red peppers from a jar, finely
  chopped
300ml (½ pint) buttermilk, or
  150ml (¼ pint) milk mixed with
  150ml (¼ pint) natural yogurt
oil for greasing

Makes 1 loaf
Preheat your oven to 200°C (400°F), Gas Mark 6. Put all the dry ingredients in a large bowl and mix well. Add the peppers and stir again, then add the buttermilk or milk/yogurt mixture and stir until everything is well combined and you have a sticky dough. Tip out onto a greased baking tray, shape into a round loaf and cut a deep cross in the top. Cook for 30–45 minutes until you get that reassuring hollow sound when you tap its bottom.

BREAKFASTS FOR AUTUMN

These are dishes that truly celebrate the bounties of the season, with all its colours and earthy flavours. Breakfasts to savour, not to rush.

Mushrooms on Toast

There are certain things that I will always associate with my grandmother, Paddy. Rich Tea biscuits, which she would have with her morning tea before she got up. House coats. Chocolate buttons. Gin and tonic. And, curiously, mushrooms on toast. I say curiously, because I can't actually remember her ever making them for me, but for reasons long forgotten, she and that glorious smell of mushrooms frying in butter are synonymous.

I would love to say that I spend every autumn morning out in the fields foraging the mushrooms I then cook up for breakfast, but it would be a lie. My knowledge of mushrooms is woeful and my fear of picking, cooking and eating something that looks innocuous but is actually deadly is – reassuringly for everyone I hold dear – enough to stop me trying. Every year I promise myself I will join my brilliant mushroom expert friend Simon on a forage, and then time does its thing, and the season is over once again.

So, you can use any mushrooms you like here, foraged from your local woods and fields or from the shelves of your local supermarket. It looks like a lot of mushrooms, but they shrink a lot when cooking and they are so delicious you don't want to scrimp. Your lovely, buttery mushrooms deserve a thickish slice of toast to languish on, I think. I'd go wholemeal, but you can choose whatever you like.

a knob of butter

oil

1 garlic clove

150g (5½oz) mixed mushrooms

a good sprinkling of chopped
  parsley

crème fraîche (optional)

sea salt flakes and pepper

toast, to serve

Serves 1

Melt the butter with a glug of oil in a large frying pan over a medium heat. Crush or grate the garlic into the pan and let it soften but not brown. Cut up any of the mushrooms that are really big, but leave them quite chunky. Add them to the pan. Stir them gently every now and then so they cook evenly. They'll start to release some of that lovely, fragrant juice which mixes so deliciously with the butter.

When the mushrooms are starting to soften – after 3–4 minutes – put your toast on.

Sprinkle most of the parsley over the mushrooms (leaving some for the end) with a good pinch of sea salt flakes and a few grinds of black pepper. If you want to add crème fraîche, do it now. Turn down the heat and let the mushrooms bubble quietly until your toast is ready. It is up to you and your conscience whether you want more butter on your toast, but whatever you choose, pile on the mushrooms and all their garlicky, buttery juices, sprinkle with more parsley and tuck in.

Shakshuka

Some years ago, I was in Tel Aviv for a few weeks for work. It was here I discovered the joys of this dish, which bewitches the senses with its rich colour and aroma of warm spices. Although straightforward to make, it involves rather more chopping and cooking than most of us have the time or inclination for first thing in the morning, so you might save this for a weekend brunch. Or lunch or a light supper – it is a perfect 'any time' meal. But it is also worth noting that the eggs are added at the very last minute. The sauce can be cooked in advance and will keep for two or three days very happily in the fridge. All you have to do is heat it up, add the eggs, cook them for a few moments and it's ready. Fridge to plate in 10–12 minutes, I reckon. This dish is easiest cooked in a large sauté pan with a lid.

½ teaspoon coriander seeds
½ teaspoon cumin seeds
olive oil
1 onion, sliced into half moons
1 garlic clove
1 teaspoon thyme leaves
2 peppers (any colour), sliced
1–2 teaspoons sugar
6 tomatoes, roughly chopped,

or a 400g (14oz) can chopped
  tomatoes
a handful of chopped parsley
a handful of chopped fresh
  coriander
cayenne pepper or chipotle flakes
  (optional)
4 large eggs
salt and pepper

Serves 4
Dry-fry the coriander and cumin seeds in a pan until lightly toasted, then tip into a pestle and mortar and crush them, just to break them up a bit. Heat a glug of oil in a large sauté pan over a medium heat. Add the onion and cook until soft but not brown. Grate in the garlic clove and add the thyme leaves,

slices of pepper and the sugar and cook for another few minutes until the peppers start to soften.

Add the tomatoes, the crushed cumin and coriander seeds and most of the chopped parsley and fresh coriander, leaving some for garnish at the end. Season with salt, black pepper and a shake of cayenne pepper or a pinch or 2 of chipotle flakes if you want some heat. Cook on a low heat, adding a splash of water if it needs it. You want a thick, chunky sauce that tastes rich and full of flavour. This could take 10–15 minutes of slow, patient cooking. All this can be done in advance and set aside until you want it.

Once you are ready to cook the eggs, reheat the sauce then make 4 small wells in the sauce into which you break your eggs. Sprinkle them with salt, cover the pan and cook on a low heat for 8 minutes or so until the whites are cooked, but the yolks still soft. Bring to the table in its pan, sprinkled with more chopped coriander and parsley, and serve with hunks of bread for mopping.

Blackberry & Apple Compote
꙳

Blackberry picking is one of life's simplest and most rewarding of pleasures. When I was a child, our family would go for walks along the lanes and around the fields near our house, clutching bags and Tupperware boxes, to gather this beautiful fruit that heralds the start of autumn. We would return home with our bounty – fingers, lips and tongues stained purple – having eaten almost as many as we'd picked. You can find cultivated blackberries in the shops now, but they don't have the flavour of their wild relatives, they are expensive, and they don't give you the sense of satisfaction that comes with finding and gathering your own food. Blackberries freeze very well – I just put them in a bag or box whole, shove them in the freezer and get out handfuls whenever I want a hit of that sharp-sweet flavour and jewel-like colour.

This compote also freezes very well or will keep in the fridge for four or five days, so I'm not going to give you exact measurements here. Make a batch, eat it for breakfast, try my favourite childhood pudding on page 200, use it for a crumble or a fool or with pancakes, even alongside a piece of roast pork instead of bog-standard apple sauce. It's your kitchen. Anything goes.

Bramleys are the classic cooking apples, but if you have apple trees, or your neighbours do and they'll let you scrump them, any mixture of apples will work here and will give you a variety of texture as some will cook down softer than others. Peel, core and chop the apples into chunks and put them in a large saucepan. I like them to hold some of their shape, rather than cooking down to a baby food-like consistency, so I keep my chunks quite big. Add either a splash of water – and you really don't need much: apples release a lot of water when cooking and you can always add more if you need to as they cook down – or orange juice. I love the background hint of orange with apples and blackberries, so I'll zest an unwaxed orange, put the zest in with the apples, and then poach them in the juice. I'll start with the juice of just half the orange, adding the other half if needed.

Add a bit of sugar or honey – I wouldn't add much at this stage – maybe a couple of teaspoons. You can always add more later. Cook gently over a medium–low heat, stirring occasionally, and adding a bit more liquid if it needs it. The apples will start to soften and break down and – again – this bit is really up to you. Cook them for as long as they need to get the texture you like. The blackberries take moments to soften, so add them when the apples are more or less to your liking, letting that glorious juice leach out, turning the apples a regal shade of purple. Check for sweetness, adding more sugar or honey if needed.

This is better – I think anyway – not eaten when too hot, but allowed to cool off a bit. I love it just as it is, but go ahead and eat with yogurt, sprinkle some seeds or nuts on top too, or with pancakes if it is a pancake-sort-of-morning.

Poached Duck Egg on a Crumpet
with Green Chilli & Coriander

Until we starting keeping ducks, I had never eaten a duck egg. What a discovery! Encased in a thick, almost porcelain-like shell is a huge, rich, creamy yolk that looks and tastes utterly decadent. Lightly poached, it is hard to think of a more luxurious way of starting a day. And so this recipe is not only a strong contender for my favourite breakfast of all time, but could even be on my Death Row meal list. It's in competition, though, with Ludo's Cheese on Toast (see page 236), and a properly hot and excellent curry.

If you can't get hold of duck eggs, this will, of course, work with hen eggs, it just won't be quite so decadent. I've suggested – somewhat parsimoniously – one crumpet topped with one egg, but by all means double up if one doesn't seem enough.

1 good-quality crumpet	finely chopped green chilli
1 fresh duck egg	a few fresg coriander leaves,
butter	roughly chopped
Marmite (optional)	salt and pepper

Serves 1

Put a small saucepan of water on to boil. If you like your crumpet fairly crisp (I do) you might want to put it bottom side up under a hot grill now, or pop it in the toaster (but I find you need to toast it twice).

Once the water is boiling, turn it down so it is just bubbling and break the egg into the water. I like mine soft, and very fresh duck eggs cook quickly, so you've got 2–3 minutes here to get your crumpet ready. Turn it over if under the grill, or give it another bit of time in the toaster. When the crumpet is cooked to your liking, butter it and – if using – spread with Marmite. If you've never tried eggs with Marmite, it is a joyful discovery. Unless you hate Marmite.

Place your poached egg on top of the crumpet, season it well and scatter with finely chopped green chilli and roughly chopped coriander leaves. There are some dishes that require a moment of ceremony before eating and this is one. Sit at your kitchen table, with some beautiful, stirring music on in the background, and savour that moment of plunging your knife into the egg to release the golden river of yolk.

MAIN COURSES FOR AUTUMN

꘎

My autumn repertoire doesn't banish summery possibilities, like eating outside or the occasional picnic-y feast. Alongside the sort of stew you might want after a bracing walk on a windy hill, there's a salad for those warmer days, and a simple autumn feast built around the glory that is cheese.

My Favourite Autumn Salad

All the elements of this salad are delicious in their own right. Put them all together and it is as satisfying as gathering five of your favourite people around a table and creating an instant rapport. All you have to do is sit back and enjoy the ride.

Choose a strong, crumbly, smelly-as-you-dare blue cheese. I love the Welsh cheese Per Laas, and Gorgonzola or Roquefort are also good here. I'm mildly put off by overly arranged salads, but this one is worth primping just a bit.

FOR THE DRESSING

1 tablespoon olive oil

1 tablespoon walnut oil

1 tablespoon white balsamic
   vinegar

juice of ½ lemon

salt and pepper

FOR THE SALAD

a handful of walnut halves

2 heads of red endive (AKA
   chicory)

2 handfuls of watercress

2 just-ripe Conference pears

blue cheese

Serves 2

Make the dressing by whisking the oils and vinegar together, then adding lemon juice and seasoning to taste.

Toast the walnut halves in a dry frying pan until they are slightly browned.

Peel some of the outer leaves off the heads of the endive and leave them whole. Slice the rest of the endive. Remove any thick stalks from the watercress. Put the sliced endive and watercress in a bowl and dress lightly with some of the dressing, mixing with your hands so the leaves are evenly glossy but not soggy.

Cut the pears into quarters, removing the core and any pips. Crumble up as much cheese as you want to go with this. Arrange the pear quarters and whole endive leaves around the edge of a serving dish. Pile the dressed watercress and sliced endive in the middle of the dish. Scatter over the crumbled cheese and toasted walnuts and perhaps drizzle a little more dressing over everything. Take a moment to admire it, but only a moment. This is not a salad that should sit around.

Mum's Smoked Fish Pâté

I've been eating this for as long as I can remember and making it all my adult life. This pâté is so familiar, it was oddly difficult to translate it into a proper recipe, because making it is almost second nature. Yet whenever I produce it for other people, they seem to think it is something of an achievement, when, honestly, it couldn't be simpler.

200g (7oz) smoked mackerel, trout or hot-smoked salmon fillets	juice of 1 lemon
	1 teaspoon hot horseradish sauce
150g (5½oz) quark	25g (1oz) dill or parsley, chopped
150g (5½oz) cream cheese	black pepper

Serves 4

If your fish fillets have skin or bones, remove them. Break up the fish into chunks and put into a food processor. Add the quark, cream cheese, lemon juice, horseradish sauce, herbs and a good grind of black pepper. Whizz briefly – you might need to push the mixture down the sides with a spatula. Then whizz again until it is the consistency you like. Mum and I both like it to be a bit chunky, so it doesn't entirely lose the texture of the fish. This is delicious on crackers or toast or with crudités – celery, cucumber, carrot, cauliflower, radishes all work well.

A Plate of Cheese & Things to Go with It

This is a picnic, really. Something that could be eaten outside on one of those Indian summer days, but just as easily transferred to the kitchen table if the weather isn't on your side.

As cheese is the star attraction here, you might want to explore the deli counter or a local farm shop or farmers market, rather than settling for the pre-cut, pre-wrapped options – but it is, of course, entirely up to you. I love a mixture of hard and soft cheeses, maybe a goats' or a sheeps' cheese as well as cows' cheese. And definitely something blue and potent.

Alongside the cheese, I'd have bowls of crisp, peppery radishes, tomatoes, celery. There would be some simply dressed salad leaves, a dish of new season's apples. Soda bread. And then some or all of the accompaniments on the following pages.

Gazpacho

A chilled soup on an autumn day? I know – it has to be the right day – but early autumn is a time when there is often a glut of tomatoes and peppers, and gazpacho makes very fine use of them.

2 red peppers, chopped
1 cucumber, chopped (leave the skin on)
500g (1lb 2oz) ripe tomatoes, quartered
1 red or green chilli, deseeded (or not if you like the heat) and sliced

2 garlic cloves
4 spring onions, sliced
4 tablespoons olive oil
1–3 tablespoons sherry vinegar, or red wine vinegar
salt and pepper
chives, to garnish (optional)

Serves 4

Put all the vegetables into a blender with the olive oil, 1 tablespoon of the vinegar and a generous amount of salt and pepper. Blend until smooth. Taste and add more vinegar and seasoning if you think it needs it.

As part of a picnic, I'd serve this not in bowls (with finely chopped cucumber, tomato and spring onion as a garnish, ice cubes floating in it and an extra trickle of olive oil on top), but in glass tumblers with chopped chives on the top, to drink, rather than eat with a spoon. Which might be a bit common, but I don't care.

Bloody Mary

Less work than gazpacho, but as good, is a beautifully spiced and seasoned jug of tomato juice, with or without vodka and sherry. If you'd rather have Bloody (or Virgin) Marys instead, here is an approximation of Ludo's tomato juice mix.

I say approximation, because he just shakes bottles and jars over the top of a jug, so there are no precise measurements here. You'll know when it tastes right.

500ml (18fl oz) tomato juice   lemon juice

Worcestershire sauce   celery salt

Tabasco sauce   black pepper

Serves 2

Put the tomato juice in a jug. Add a few shakes of Worcestershire sauce, 4–5 drops of Tabasco, a good squeeze of lemon juice, a generous pinch of celery salt and a grinding or 2 of black pepper. Then stir, taste and add more of anything you think it might need. Serve in big glasses with ice, a stick of celery and a slice of lemon, if you like.

For a boozier version, add vodka – Nina and Joe of the Silver Circle Distillery make a black garlic vodka which is ridiculously good in this – and a shot of sherry or Chilli Sherry (see page 149), which is not 100 per cent necessary, but an excellent addition if you have it.

Jo's Membrillo

Our neighbours down the hill, Mark and Jo, have some fabulously productive quince trees in their garden and every autumn Jo will bring me some of the wonderful membrillo – also known as quince cheese – that she makes.

Quinces don't look very appetizing – a bit like yellow apples with a skin condition – and they can't be eaten raw. But, like rhubarb, they work really well with savoury dishes, added to meaty stews or tagines. You can also poach them with sugar and spices to serve on porridge or with yogurt, make them into a tart or add them to apples or pears in a crumble. But membrillo, which is a fragrant, slightly grainy fruit preserve from Spain that is solid enough to slice, is wonderful served with cheese and charcuterie.

It is easiest to make this over two days. Cook the quinces on the first day and make the membrillo the following day.

500g (1lb 2oz) quinces

250–400g (9–14oz) granulated sugar

Makes about 500g (1lb 2oz)

Wash and roughly chop the quinces, but don't peel them or remove the cores. Put in a large pan and add water until the fruit is just covered. Bring to the boil and simmer until the quinces have become soft and started to collapse. You may need to add more water during the cooking process. Once they are done, leave them in the pan in their water overnight.

The next day, push the contents of the pan through a sieve into a bowl. Weigh the resulting pulp, then return it to the washed-up pan with an equal weight of sugar. Bring to the boil, stirring to dissolve the sugar, then turn down the heat and simmer for about an hour, stirring frequently. You want the mixture to become really thick and shiny. It's ready when you drag the spoon through the mixture and you can see the bottom of the pan for a few seconds before the mixture oozes back and covers it again.

Line a shallow baking tray with a long enough piece of baking paper that you can fold the excess back over the top of the membrillo. Scrape in the mixture and smooth it out so you have a large rectangle of thick, deep orange paste. Cover over with the baking paper and store in the fridge. The next day you can cut it into smaller pieces and wrap each one in baking paper, before returning to the fridge. Like many preserves, it is best left for 4–6 weeks before using, but it will keep in the fridge for a year and it does make lovely presents!

Amie's Chilli Jam

I have, as you may have gathered, a penchant for chillies. Not only do I love eating them, they are also gratifyingly easy to grow – even for someone as un-green-fingered as me. In fact, so easy are they that I often end up with more chillies than even I know what to do with.

My dear friend Amie came to the rescue one year by taking away a large bag full of chillies I had grown and returning with jars full of brightly glistening chilli jam. It seemed like a pretty unfair swap, so I begged her for the recipe so I could make my own and give her some jars in return. The lovely thing about this jam is that you can eat it pretty much immediately – you don't need to wait for it to mature like many chutneys, and its gorgeous, gently potent flavour goes beautifully with almost anything from cheese to cold meat, to sausages, roast chicken…

150g (5½oz) red chillies, deseeded and roughly chopped (keep some of the seeds if you like a bit of extra heat)

150g (5½oz) red pepper, roughly chopped

1kg (2lb 4oz) jam sugar

600ml (20fl oz) cider vinegar

Makes about 5 jars

Have some sterilized jars standing by – I'd do 7 or 8 just in case. Wash them and then put in a baking tray in the oven at 140°C (275°F), Gas Mark 1 to dry. They can sit there while you make your jam.

Pulse the chillies and red peppers together in a food processor until they are very finely chopped. Dissolve the sugar in the vinegar in a large pan over a low heat without stirring. Add the chillies and peppers, stir in and bring to the boil. Let sit at a rollicking boil for 10 minutes, then take it off the hob and let it cool for about 5 minutes. Then ladle into your warm jars.

Penny's Irresistible Chutney
with Green Tomatoes & Apples

Fred Astaire and Ginger Rogers. Torvill and Dean. Cheese and Chutney. You can't have one without the other. And this heavenly concoction of green tomatoes, apples and spices is a perfect partner for cheese. The only annoying thing is, like all chutneys, it needs to sit in a cool, dark place in its jars for 6 weeks to mature before eating. Sorry.

700g (1lb 9oz) green tomatoes, chopped

500g (1lb 2oz) apples (cookers or eaters), peeled, cored and chopped

2 onions, chopped

50g (1¾oz) sultanas

½ teaspoon peeled and grated fresh ginger

1 long red chilli, thinly sliced (seeds optional depending on whether you like the heat)

¼ teaspoon grated nutmeg

¼ teaspoon ground white pepper

¼ teaspoon ground allspice

½ teaspoon salt

175g (6oz) granulated sugar

450ml (16fl oz) malt vinegar

Makes about 4 jars

Put all of the ingredients – except for the sugar and 350ml (12fl oz) of the vinegar – into a large saucepan. Bring to the boil and simmer gently, stirring occasionally, for about 30–45 minutes.

Add the sugar and the remaining vinegar and stir over a low heat until the sugar has dissolved. Bring to the boil and boil rapidly until thickened, while stirring to avoid it catching. Spoon into warm, dry, sterilized jars (see page 227) and seal immediately, using jam covers to prevent the vinegar from corroding the lids. Store in a cool, dark place.

And Her Famous Oatcakes

I know you can buy oatcakes everywhere, but honestly, if you are ever struck by a need to bake something – bake these! They are less solid than shop-bought oatcakes, a bit more crumbly and properly delicious, even just on their own without the benefit of a hunk of cheese. This dough also freezes well or you can freeze the uncooked oatcakes between layers of baking paper, ready to go straight into the oven when you need them.

100g (3½oz) butter, softened

35g (1¼oz) granulated or demerara
  sugar

100g (3½oz) rolled oats

50g (1¾oz) plain flour, plus extra
  for dusting

a pinch of salt

1 tablespoon finely ground oatmeal
  for topping (optional)

Makes 14–20, depending on size

Beat together the butter and sugar until pale and creamy. Then add the oats, flour and salt and mix together well. With your hands, squash the mixture together to form a ball, wrap it in clingfilm and chill in the fridge for 20 minutes.

Preheat your oven to 160°C (325°F), Gas Mark 3, and line a baking tray with a reusable nonstick liner or baking paper. Once it has had its time in the fridge, roll out the dough on a lightly floured surface until it is about 6–7mm (a generous ¼in) thick. Cut into rounds or fingers and sprinkle with oatmeal, if you like. Any offcuts can be rerolled.

Place on your prepared baking tray and cook for 18–20 minutes until lightly coloured. They are very fragile when hot, so leave to cool for a few minutes before placing on a wire rack.

The Ultimate BLT

There are few things gloomier than an over-chilled, tasteless, shop-bought sandwich in a triangular packet. And the prize for the nastiest of them all has to go to the BLT, with its cold bit of bacon, slimy lettuce, woolly tomato and watery mayonnaise. A homemade one, with warm, freshly cooked bacon, will outshine anything you can buy, but one that includes bacon you have cured yourself and your very own mayonnaise is nothing short of a culinary masterpiece.

We met Graham Waddington not long after we moved to Wales. We had raised a couple of young pigs, or weaners as they are known, and the time came for them to be slaughtered. You can, you will be told if you ever raise pigs for your own table, eat every part of a pig apart from the squeal. But if you have only ever bought ready-butchered cuts, as we had up until

then, a whole pig is a daunting prospect and there were many bits we had no idea what to do with.

Graham and his wife Ruth run an artisan charcuterie business. Charcuterie is meat that has been dried or cured or processed in some way – things like salami, ham and bacon. To do it well is an art that must be learned over a lifetime, but Graham taught us a simple way to cure bacon, which anyone can do at home, whether you raise your own pigs or not. The only ingredients you need that you might not already have in your cupboard are curing salt and ascorbic acid, but both can be bought very easily online.

Start to finish, the process takes 8–10 days, but needs no specialist equipment and you will, I promise, end up with the best bacon you have ever tasted. Graham advocates using pork belly because if you have never cured bacon before it is the easiest cut to work with and to slice once cured. And it also has a better flavour than pork loin, because it is fattier. The resulting bacon makes an excellent ingredient in cooking as well as on its own (see the recipe for Bacon Jam on page 182).

Homemade Bacon

You can use just the ingredients in the top list, or add all or any of the optional ingredients listed below to your cure.

1-kg (2lb 4-oz) piece of pork belly
   (rind on or off, it's up to you)
40g (1½oz) curing salt
30g (1oz) demerara sugar

5g (⅛oz) ascorbic acid
4g (scant ⅛oz) ground white
   pepper

OPTIONAL INGREDIENTS
8g (scant ¼oz) juniper berries,
   coarsely ground
10g (¼oz) coarsely ground black
   pepper

8g (scant ¼oz) dried rosemary
5g (⅛oz) garlic powder
3 dried bay leaves, shredded
10g (¼oz) white mustard seeds

Makes 1kg (2lb 4oz)

Put your piece of pork belly onto a baking tray. Mix all the remaining ingredients together in a bowl to make the cure. Rub the cure all over the piece of pork belly, ensuring it is evenly covered. Then wrap it tightly in clingfilm to ensure all the cure remains on the meat. Leave it in the fridge for 4–5 days.

Once it has had its curing time, take it out of the fridge and wash it thoroughly under a cold tap to remove all the cure then dry with kitchen paper. Put it, uncovered, on a rack in the fridge (a grill pan with its rack works well) for another 3–5 days. Then it's ready to slice and use. And don't feel you have to get a fancy meat slicer – a carving knife is fine. You'll end up with slightly thicker slices of bacon, but it is so delicious you won't care. Wrapped in clingfilm, the bacon will keep for 10 days in the fridge.

Homemade Mayonnaise

Making mayonnaise was, I believed, something of a dark art. Turns out it really isn't, and homemade mayonnaise does taste very different – in a good way – to the ready-made stuff. I use an electric hand whisk to do the whisking, which somehow makes it less stressful. Use whatever oil you like – I find that 200ml (7fl oz) of olive oil and 300ml (½ pint) of sunflower oil is a nice mix.

2 egg yolks	juice of ½ lemon
1 heaped teaspoon Dijon mustard	2 tablespoons white wine vinegar
a pinch each of salt and white pepper	500ml (18fl oz) oil

Serves 6–8

In a bowl or wide jug, whisk the egg yolks, mustard, salt, pepper, lemon juice and 1 tablespoon of the vinegar until well combined. Keep whisking while slowly drizzling in half the oil.

Then add the remaining vinegar (this helps to prevent splitting). Continue slowly adding in oil and whisking until the mixture thickens to become the familiar silky texture of mayonnaise. Check if it needs any extra seasoning. Any leftover mayo will keep in the fridge for up to 5 days, stored in a clean, airtight jar.

Mayonnaise Trouble-shooting

If the mayonnaise is too thick, just whisk in a tablespoon of boiling water – this will also make the mayonnaise taste less oily.

If it does curdle while you are whisking, pour the mixture into another bowl and thoroughly wash your mixing bowl. Separate another egg and put the yolk into the newly washed bowl and gradually whisk your original mixture back in.

Bacon Jam

When Angharad said she was going to show me how to make bacon jam, I thought I'd misheard her, or that she had slightly lost the plot. I know she can turn most things into a preserve, but bacon? Really? But believe me, it works. Think a bacon version of 'nduja.

Bacon jam is better known in the United States, where it is sometimes made with a splash of bourbon. Angharad has used mead in her recipe, because there are a couple of local guys who make beautiful mead, but you can use either, or whisky, or no alcohol at all. Give it a go! It's a great thing to use your home-cured bacon for and there are suggestions below of what you might do with it.

500g (1lb 2oz) smoked bacon
   lardons
1 large onion, finely sliced
2 garlic cloves, crushed
50g (1¾oz) light brown sugar
2 tablespoons cider vinegar

2 tablespoons honey
100ml (3½fl oz) freshly brewed
   strong black coffee
1 tablespoon mead (or bourbon or
   whisky)

Makes 2 jars

Fry the bacon in a large nonstick pan for 5–10 minutes until crisp and golden. Remove with a slotted spoon and set aside, leaving the fat in the pan.

Turn down the heat and cook the onion in the bacon fat for 15–20 minutes until soft and starting to brown. Stir in the garlic, sugar, cider vinegar, honey and coffee and return the bacon to the pan. Cook slowly for 20–30 minutes, stirring occasionally, until thick and syrupy. Turn off the heat, add the mead (or whatever you are using) and leave to cool for a few minutes. Then tip the whole lot into a food processor. Pulse briefly to chop into small pieces then pack the bacon jam into 2 sterilized jars (see page 226) or a sealable tub. It will keep for a month in the fridge.

⤻

Bacon Jam is delicious on crackers, as a condiment on burgers or in a toasted cheese sandwich, but it is particularly heavenly with roast chicken. The recipe that follows is for a spatchcocked chicken. Until very recently I would never have cooked a recipe that demanded spatchcocking a chicken because I had no idea how to do it. But it is a great trick, because it just about halves the cooking time of a roast chicken. And it is gratifyingly easy to do, I have now learned. I'll talk you through it.

However, if it still feels a bit daunting or you don't have a pair of poultry shears or good, strong kitchen scissors, you can still cook this. Just leave your chicken whole, push the bacon jam under the skin on the breast and cook it for longer, until the juices run clear when you poke a skewer between the breast and the legs.

Spatchcocked Chicken
with Bacon Jam

1 chicken, about 1.8kg (4lb)	olive oil
100g (3½oz) Bacon Jam	salt and pepper

Serves 4–6

Preheat your oven to 200°C (400°F), Gas Mark 6. Put your chicken on a chopping board with the cavity facing towards you. Turn it upside down, so the breast is on the board and the flat side of the chicken is facing upwards. There is a triangular wedge of skin – like an arrowhead – pointing towards you. That is known as the parson's nose (not very flattering if you happen to be a parson).

Running in a straight line behind the parson's nose is the chicken's backbone and this is what you want to remove.

Take your poultry shears or kitchen scissors and, directly along one side of the parson's nose, start to cut in a straight line away from you until you reach the other end of the chicken. You will be cutting through some bones, so expect this to be a little crunchy, but it doesn't need huge force to be able to do it. Make a second cut starting on the other side of the parson's nose perpendicular to the first cut. You will then have freed the backbone, which should come away in one long piece. Remove it and keep for stock if you like.

Now turn your chicken back over, place your hand on the breast and push down firmly to flatten the bird. You will hear a small, satisfying crack as the wishbone gives way. You have now spatchcocked your chicken!

Put it on a baking tray lined with baking paper, skin side up. Spread out the legs so it is lying as flat as possible. Loosen the skin over the breast by easing your fingers underneath it and then stuff in the bacon jam, easing it under the skin as far you can reach, trying to get an even spread. Rub some oil into the skin and season with salt and pepper and then put it in the oven to roast for about 45 minutes. Check it's cooked by piercing the inside of the legs. If the juices run clear, it is ready. Let it rest for about 10 minutes before serving.

This chicken is delicious just with a big green salad and a hunk of Soda Bread or a baked potato, but if it is a cold, wet day and you want something warm and colourful to go with it, or just a substantial vegetarian option to serve alongside the chicken, you can't go far wrong with a Roasted Ratatouille. Handily it cooks in the same amount of time as the chicken, so you can do the whole lot together and put your feet up with a cuppa and a crossword until they are ready.

Roasted Ratatouille

1 aubergine, cut into generous
  chunks
2 courgettes, cut into chunks
1 large red onion, cut into wedges
2–3 peppers (a mix of colours is
  nice), cut into chunks
a small bunch of parsley, roughly
  chopped

leaves from 6 sprigs of thyme
olive oil
chilli flakes (optional)
200g (7oz) cherry tomatoes on the
  vine
1 whole head of garlic, sliced in half
  along its 'equator'
salt and pepper

Serves 4–6

Preheat your oven to 200°C (400°F), Gas Mark 6. Put the aubergine,
courgettes, onion, peppers, parsley and thyme into a large baking dish or

roasting tin. Drizzle with olive oil and season
well with salt and pepper and a good pinch of
chilli flakes it you want a little bit of heat. Mix
everything around so the vegetables are evenly
coated in oil and seasoning. Place the vines of
cherry tomatoes and the garlic halves, cut side
up, on top of the vegetables, drizzle both with a
bit more oil and a sprinkling of salt and pepper
and put in the oven.

Roast for about 45 minutes until the
vegetables are tender and slightly coloured.
Serve warm, passing around the garlic so your
guests can squeeze the delicious, soft cloves
from the skin.

Three Ways with Your Ratatouille

As well as a delicious side dish, you can turn this ratatouille into various vegetarian main courses.

With pasta – Once the vegetables are cooked, stir through some cooked pasta and add a big handful of fresh chopped herbs and grated cheese.

On sourdough – Toast a slice of sourdough, heap a generous amount of warm or room temperature ratatouille on top and crumble over feta and ripped-up basil leaves.

In soup – Put the cooked vegetables into a blender and blitz with a bit of stock to make a quick, really flavoursome soup.

Curry: a Short Eulogy

Working in India, Sri Lanka and Nepal over the years, I became sort of addicted to curries. To the point where I would happily eat curry for every meal. I tend to favour vegetarian curries, or think I do, and then will have a delicate, fragrant fish curry or robust, deeply flavoured mutton curry, and remember again that magical way a clever combination of spices transforms and enhances almost anything.

Despite the macho beliefs of some, curry isn't all about heat. I don't have any desire to eat food that makes my eyes water, my nose run and my lips burn. But I love the excitement, the thrill of the intricate layers of tastes and flavours you can get from a good curry. Last year, when I was staying with my friends Sarah and Tracey, they made their version of a curry that I cook time and time again. And it was spectacular. Rather better than mine. So, this is their recipe. Thank you, lovelies!

Tomato Curry

You need a large sauté pan for this dish, or two large frying pans. Use a mixture of tomatoes if you can – Tracey uses 1kg (2lb 4oz) of vine tomatoes and 200g (7oz) of yellow plum tomatoes because it makes the dish look very pretty!

1 teaspoon fennel seeds

1 teaspoon black mustard seeds

1 teaspoon cumin seeds

1 teaspoon coriander seeds

5 tablespoons rapeseed oil

10 cardamom pods, lightly crushed

2 onions, sliced into half moons

16 curry leaves

1.2kg (2lb 12oz) mixed tomatoes

1–2 green chillies, finely chopped

4 garlic cloves, crushed

3 teaspoons tamarind paste

400ml (14fl oz) can coconut milk

salt

a handful of fresh coriander and
    lime juice (optional), to serve

Serves 4

In your large sauté pan, toast the fennel, mustard, cumin and coriander seeds until they are warm and fragrant. Tip into a pestle and mortar and grind until fairly fine. In the same sauté pan, heat 4 tablespoons of the rapeseed oil over a medium heat, add the ground spices, the cardamom pods, the onions, 8 curry leaves and 1½ teaspoons of salt. Fry for 10–12 minutes until the onions are golden. In the meantime, cut up your tomatoes. I just halve them, but you can cut them up smaller if you prefer.

Add the chillies and garlic to the pan and cook, stirring for a couple of minutes, before adding the tamarind and coconut milk. Stir so everything is well combined, then add the tomatoes. They need to sit in a single layer in the pan, so if you think your pan won't be big enough, divide your sauce between 2 pans and then add the tomatoes.

On a low–medium heat, let the tomatoes sit in the beautiful spiced mixture, cooking gently so they soften as the water in the coconut milk evaporates, leaving you with a rich, reduced sauce. This will take about 20 minutes. While waiting, heat the remaining oil in a small pan and fry your remaining curry leaves so they crackle and crisp, then set aside on kitchen paper.

Once the curry is ready, check for seasoning – it might need a bit more salt – then scatter with coriander leaves and the crispy curry leaves. I quite like it with a squeeze of lime juice too. Serve with rice or chapattis and some coconut yogurt. A spiky lime pickle is also good, as is the glorious Sambal on page 244.

Brazilian Fish Stew

I first ate this dish not in Brazil but in my friend Kirsty's kitchen. It is inspired by *moqueca*, a Brazilian seafood stew, and it tastes wonderful. It is also one of those brilliantly convenient things to cook when you have friends over. You can prepare almost all of it in advance, so you don't have to be working away in the kitchen while everyone else is knocking back the wine and catching up without you. I use a mix of white fish and prawns, but you can use just fish or just prawns.

500g (1lb 2oz) firm white fish

450g (1lb) raw peeled prawns

zest and juice of 2 unwaxed limes

3 garlic cloves, finely chopped

3 tablespoons coconut oil

1 onion, thinly sliced into half
　　moons

1 red pepper, sliced

1 green pepper, sliced

4 spring onions, sliced

1 teaspoon chilli flakes

1 teaspoon paprika

3 tomatoes, deseeded and chopped

400ml (14fl oz) can coconut milk

salt and pepper

a handful of fresh coriander and
　　lime wedges, to serve

Serves 4–6

Chop the fish into bite-sized chunks and put in a bowl with the prawns. Pour over the lime juice and sprinkle with the zest, half the chopped garlic and a teaspoon of salt. Mix and let marinate for an hour or so.

While the fish is marinating you can get on with the rest of the stew, because it can happily sit until you are ready to eat – you just heat it up and add the fish just before you want to serve it. The fish will cook in moments.

Heat the coconut oil in a large saucepan over a medium heat and gently fry the onion until it is translucent. Add the peppers and cook for 2–3 minutes, then add the spring onions along with the remaining garlic, the chilli flakes and paprika. Occasionally push them gently around the pan so nothing sticks. Once the smell of garlic and paprika starts to rise from the pan, add the chopped tomatoes and coconut milk and simmer gently for 10 minutes.

You can then leave it covered on the hob, or cool it and put it in the fridge, until you want to eat. Or you can carry on and add the fish and the prawns straight away. If you have made the sauce in advance, reheat it gently until it comes back to a simmer, add the fish and prawns in their marinade and stir gently until the fish has turned opaque and the prawns pink – about 3–4 minutes. Season with salt and pepper. Serve scattered with coriander, with lime wedges for squeezing.

Feel the Beet...

Beetroot was – and still is to some extent – one of those things that school dinners ruined for me. But I'm slowly coming around to its earthy charms, partly because it is gratifyingly easy to grow and, roasted slowly, it is an entirely different thing from the pickled stuff that was a staple part of my school diet.

I still can't abide pickled beetroot and its lurid, vinegary juice that turns everything pink, but the recipe that is coming up is the one that has made me properly understand why so many people love beetroot. It was given to us for lunch by Maryann Wright who, together with her husband Simon, runs one of my favourite places to eat in the world. It's called Wright's Food Emporium and, if you ever find yourself in Carmarthenshire in West Wales, seek it out. Maryann has generously shared a couple of her wonderful recipes with me and this is one of them.

Beet Bourguignon

1 large onion, diced

2 garlic cloves, finely chopped

1 thumb-sized piece of ginger, peeled and finely chopped

1 red chilli, finely chopped

olive oil

200g (7oz) chestnut mushrooms, sliced

1 teaspoon smoked paprika

1 tablespoon tomato purée

250ml (9fl oz) red wine

1kg (2lb 4oz) mixed beetroot

250g (9oz) rainbow carrots

150g (5½oz) dried green lentils

250ml (9fl oz) vegetable stock (fresh or from a cube)

1 sprig of thyme

4 bay leaves

salt and pepper

a bunch of flat leaf parsley, chopped, to serve

Serves 4–6

Sauté the onion, garlic, ginger and chilli in a little olive oil in a large saucepan or casserole dish until soft. Add the mushrooms to the pan with the paprika and cook for about 5 minutes, then add the tomato purée and red wine and simmer until reduced by about one-third.

Peel and chop the beetroot and the carrots into roughly even-sized chunks and add to the pan. Cook for 10 minutes, then add the lentils, stock, thyme and bay leaves and simmer until the lentils have softened but still have some bite. Season to taste and serve sprinkled with chopped parsley.

I don't think this needs anything with it; a hunk of your Autumn Soda Bread, perhaps (see page 156), but no one is going to complain if you serve it with mash.

The Perfect Autumn Stew
with Pork, Apple & Cider

I love this classic combination of pork, sage and apple, cooked to melting softness with the help of a bottle of local cider. It needs no more than a warm bowl, a spoon and a hunk of bread, but if mash is called for (as it often is), a mix of potato and celeriac is particularly good. I'd also wilt down some kale to serve alongside.

sunflower oil or dripping

1kg (2lb 4oz) pork shoulder or collar, diced

3–4 onions, sliced

3 garlic cloves, thinly sliced

8–10 sage leaves

6 apples, peeled, cored and coarsely chopped

1 heaped tablespoon plain flour

1 small tablespoon English or French mustard

500ml (18fl oz) pork or chicken stock (fresh or from a cube)

500ml (18fl oz) cider

salt and pepper

Serves 4–6

Preheat your oven to 170°C (325°F), Gas Mark 3. In a large saucepan or casserole, brown the pork in the oil or dripping until there is a bit of colour on it, but not too much or it will become dry and chewy. Remove from the pan with a slotted spoon and keep warm. Fry the onions and garlic gently in the same pan until light brown.

Put the pork back in the pan with the onions and garlic, then add the sage, half the apples, the flour, mustard and seasoning and mix together. Pour in the stock and cider slowly, stirring to incorporate the flour. Let it come to the boil briefly, then cover with foil or a lid and put into the oven to cook gently.

After 1½ hours, take out your by-now-fragrant stew and add the remaining apples. See if it needs more salt and pepper and check that the meat is tender. Pop it back in the oven for another 10–15 minutes, until the newly added apples are soft. You can eat it straight away, or keep it in the fridge for a day or two, which will make it taste even better. Or you can freeze it.

Mr Brock's Ingenious Frozen Apple Crumble Ice Cream
with Blackberry Ripple

This, Freddie told me, took some work to get right, but now it is his mum's favourite. There are four elements to this ice cream – the custard base, a caramelized apple purée to flavour it, a blackberry coulis for rippling and a crumble topping.

FOR THE CUSTARD BASE

6 egg yolks (save the whites to
   make meringues)
200g (7oz) caster sugar

3 tablespoons skimmed milk powder
1 litre (1¾ pints) whole milk
150ml (¼ pint) double cream

FOR THE CARAMELIZED APPLE PURÉE

900g (2lb) cooking apples
50g (1¾oz) butter

50g (1¾oz) granulated sugar
zest of 1 unwaxed lemon

Serves 8–10

Whisk the egg yolks, sugar and skimmed milk powder together until smooth and pale. Put the milk and the cream in a saucepan and heat until bubbles form at the side but it doesn't actually boil. Take the pan off the heat and pour it into the egg mixture. Have your pot-washer thoroughly clean the pan while you stir. Then pour the mixture back into the pan, return it to a gentle heat and warm until it reaches 75°C (167°F). Take it off the heat and let it cool. Once it has cooled, chill it in the fridge overnight.

In the meantime, make the caramelized apple purée. Peel, core and chop the apples into quarters or thick slices if they are very big. Melt the butter in a frying pan, add the sugar and stir until it dissolves. Add the apples and the lemon zest in a single layer and let them bubble away, turning once, until the apples are soft and the liquid starts to brown. Scoop the soft, golden caramelized apples into a blender and whizz into a thick purée. Cool and then refrigerate overnight.

FOR THE BLACKBERRY COULIS

250g (9oz) blackberries   50g (1¾oz) caster sugar

Put the blackberries and the sugar into a pan and simmer until the blackberries soften. You may need to add a splash of water, but you'll probably find the blackberries ooze enough juice that you don't need to.

Once the blackberries are nicely soft, push them through a sieve set over a bowl to get rid of the seeds and form a purée. Return to the pan and simmer the purée for a bit longer to make a thickish syrup. Let it cool and set aside.

FOR THE CRUMBLE TOPPING

110g (3¾oz) fridge-cold butter   50g (1¾oz) soft brown sugar
170g (6oz) plain flour

Preheat your oven to 180°C (350°F), Gas Mark 4, and line a baking tray with baking paper. Cut the butter into small cubes and put in a food processor with the flour. Whizz until you have something that looks like damp sand, then add the sugar and pulse until it is well mixed in.

Pour the mixture onto the baking tray, spread it out and cook for about 15–20 minutes until golden. Check it about half way through the cooking time and break up the mixture a bit into smaller clumps. When it's done, take it out of the oven, break it up a bit more and let it cool.

When you are ready to assemble this amazing creation, you will need a 900-g (2-lb) loaf tin. Stir your caramelized apple purée into the custard base and churn in an ice cream-maker until it is softly frozen. Scoop out one-third of the ice cream mixture into the loaf tin to form a layer on the bottom. Pour half your blackberry coulis on top of the ice cream.

Top with another layer of ice cream, the rest of the blackberry, and then fill the tin with the remaining apple ice cream. Take a skewer, poke it to the bottom of one corner of the loaf tin and drag it through the mixture in a figure of 8, just once, rippling the blackberry coulis through the apple ice cream.

Put the loaf tin in the freezer to freeze the ice cream, taking it out and putting it in the fridge for 30 minutes before you want to eat it. When you do, dip the loaf tin briefly in hot water to allow you to tip the ice cream out onto a plate or board. Cut it into thick slices and serve with a generous sprinkling of the crumble on top. And some fresh blackberries if you feel like it.

PUDDINGS FOR AUTUMN

Autumn fruit makes puddings a true joy at this time of year – and I say that even as someone who is not really a pudding kind of girl.

Blackberry & Apple Meringue

This was, hands down, my favourite childhood pudding. Mum always made it in a round, white ceramic dish and the meringue, lightly browned and crisp, would stand proud of the top. And we would watch, with a sort of horrified delight, as Mum plunged her spoon through the meringue to scoop up the soft, warm fruit beneath. There is something about the contrast in textures and the sweetness of the meringue with the slight tartness of the apple and blackberry that makes this pretty perfect as puddings go.

3 cooking apples

100g (3½oz) blackberries (fresh or frozen)

2 eggs, separated

75g (2¾oz) demerara sugar, plus extra for the fruit (optional)

Serves 4

Peel, core and chop the apples and put them in a pan with a little bit of water. Cook over a medium heat until they are soft and you can break them into a purée with a wooden spoon. Add the blackberries to the pan and stir them gently in with the apple purée. You can let them cook until they purée down too, but I like the blackberries to keep their shape a bit. Taste for sweetness. Something I've inherited from Mum is a love of slightly sour, sharp flavours, so neither of us would add sugar at this stage, partly because the meringue is sweet, but you may want to.

Let the purée cool and then stir in the egg yolks – don't think you can do this while the purée is still warm because you'll end up with scrambled eggs and fruit purée. It might taste alright, but I doubt it.

Preheat your oven to 150°C (300°F), Gas Mark 2. Whisk the egg whites with an electric whisk until they form stiff peaks. Then whisk in the sugar, a tablespoon at a time. Put the fruit into an ovenproof baking dish, cover with the meringue and put in the oven. You want (well, I do) a crisp meringue – not a soggy, chewy one – so you will probably want to leave it for 50 minutes or so before you take it out. You can always check and give it a little tap to see how it's doing. Eat warm, with cream or ice cream or yogurt, or just gloriously unadorned.

The Wonder of Lemon Curd

There is something retro about lemon curd. I associate it with the era of sandwich spread and fish paste. I have vague, not altogether pleasant, memories of lemon curd sandwiches – white bread with gloopy yellow stuff in the middle. I think at least 30 years went by before I even thought about lemon curd again. But it's good, especially homemade. Better still, I've discovered some far better uses for it than sandwiches, including the two almost-instant puddings on the following pages. But first, here's how you make it. If you only have waxed lemons, just pop them in hot water for a minute and give them a rub with a cloth.

Lemon Curd

zest and juice of 2 unwaxed lemons

100g (3½oz) caster sugar

50g (1¾oz) butter

2 large eggs, beaten

Makes 2–3 jars

Put the lemon zest, juice, sugar and butter in a heatproof bowl over a pan of simmering water and allow to melt and dissolve slowly, stirring occasionally. Once the sugar has dissolved, pour in the beaten eggs, stirring all the time, and continue cooking until it becomes thick and coats the back of the spoon – a smooth custard consistency. Pour into warm sterilized jars (see page 226). This will keep for about a month but, once opened, keep in the fridge and eat within a week.

Lemon Curd Mousse
with Blackberries

500ml (18fl oz) Greek yogurt

1–2 tablespoons lemon curd

zest of 1 unwaxed lemon, juice of ½

blackberries or any other berries,

or a mixture

1 teaspoon caster sugar

mint leaves, to decorate (optional)

Serves 4

Tip your Greek yogurt into a bowl. Add a tablespoon or two of lemon curd, then taste it to see if it has the lemonyness you like. Stir in the lemon zest. Serve alongside a spoonful of berries that have been spritzed with lemon juice and sprinkled with just a teaspoon or so of sugar. A few scattered mint leaves, if you have them, look and taste nice with this.

Instant Lemon Curd Tarts
with Edible Flowers

You can buy ready-made mini sweet pastry tart cases, or make your own for this. Choose whatever edible flowers you can find – nasturtiums, marigolds, pansies, rose petals, lavender sprigs.

lemon curd   edible flowers, to decorate
4 individual tart cases

Serves 4
Spoon lemon curd into the tart cases and decorate with fresh flowers. These look really pretty, taste wonderful and take about a minute to make.

Bakewell Tart
with Fresh Autumn Raspberries

Jennifer – my friend and bread-making guru – invited us to climb the mountain behind her house. It was one of those truly special autumn afternoons – golden sunshine, deep blue skies, cold enough for a jumper but no need for a coat. We stood on the summit, glorying in the grandeur of the view that unfurled around us, then descended to her garden for tea in the late-afternoon sun. 'I made a Bakewell tart,' she said, emerging from the kitchen door with a laden tray. 'We've had such a bumper crop of raspberries I thought this would be a nice way of using some of them.' I didn't confess that Bakewell tart was something I had little fondness for, but this was unlike any Bakewell tart I had ever eaten. Light, crisp pastry, an airy, delicately almondy sponge and the sweet tang of the raspberries she had picked that morning. I begged her for the recipe and here it is.

FOR THE SHORTCRUST PASTRY

85g (3oz) unsalted butter, plus
  extra for greasing
50g (1¾oz) icing sugar
1 egg yolk, beaten
200g (7oz) plain flour, plus extra
  for dusting

FOR THE FILLING

200g (7oz) unsalted butter
200g (7oz) caster sugar
2 eggs
50g (1¾oz) self-raising flour
200g (7oz) ground almonds
good-quality raspberry jam
150g (5½oz) raspberries
50g (1¾oz) flaked almonds
icing sugar, for dusting

Serves 8

To make the pastry, cream the butter in a bowl until soft. Sift in the icing sugar and beat until fluffy. Add the beaten egg yolk and stir. Then add the flour and beat until it's all incorporated. Gather the dough in your hands, shape into a ball then flatten into a disc. Wrap in clingfilm and leave in the fridge for 30 minutes to rest.

Preheat your oven to 180°C (350°F), Gas Mark 4, and grease a 23-cm (9-in) round tart tin that's about 2.5cm (1in) deep. Roll the pastry out to a thickness of 2mm (⅟₁₆in) on a lightly floured surface and use to line the tin. Chill in the fridge for at least 30 minutes.

To make the filling, beat the butter and sugar together until light and fluffy, and then add the eggs one at a time. Mix in the flour and ground almonds and stir until you have a smooth paste.

Take your pastry-lined tin from the fridge. Smear a thin layer of raspberry jam over the bottom of the pastry case then top with the raspberries. Cover with the almond paste mixture – the filling should come right to the edges of the tin and be level. If you have a bit too much, reserve to make a mini tart! Smooth the top with a palette knife or the back of a spoon and sprinkle with flaked almonds.

Bake the tart for about 30 minutes and then cover with a piece of foil so as not to burn the flaked almonds. Bake for a further 10–15 minutes or until the filling is set and the top is golden brown. A skewer inserted into the centre should come out clean. Leave the tart to cool in the tin, then transfer to a serving plate and dust with icing sugar. The tart will keep for a week in the fridge.

Spiced Pear Crumble

There is no comfort food more comforting than a crumble. This one, with its warmly spiced, juicy pears and generous topping is perfect for this time of year.

A word about the acorn flour which is listed as an optional ingredient for the crumble topping: this is thanks to forager Liz Knight, who introduced me to the nutty, savoury splendour of this dark, flavoursome flour. It is a wonderful addition, but it is not always easy to track down. You might find it in health food shops or online, and you can make it, although it is rather more involved than I hoped. I thought you might gather a few acorns and blitz them in a coffee grinder, but no. If you want to have a go, there are various suggestions of how to do it on the internet. If you can't get hold of any and you don't have the time, inclination or acorns to make it, you could use chestnut flour, or chopped roasted hazelnuts instead.

FOR THE PEARS

125g (4½oz) granulated sugar
500ml (18fl oz) water
4 cloves
2 star anise
6 pink peppercorns
a pinch of white pepper

a pinch of ground mace
a pinch of mixed spice
a pinch of ground cinnamon
4 slightly underripe Conference
    pears

FOR THE CRUMBLE

25g (1oz) rolled oats

250g (9oz) plain flour

125g (4½oz) butter, chilled and cut
  into cubes

100g (3½oz) soft brown sugar

1 heaped tablespoon acorn flour
  (optional)

2 tablespoons flaked almonds

Serves 4–6

Preheat your oven to 180°C (350°F), Gas Mark 4. Put the sugar and water in a pan over a medium heat and stir until the sugar dissolves. Add all the spices and simmer for 2–3 minutes to infuse the syrup.

Peel, core and cut the pears into chunks then poach them in the syrup until just cooked. Remove from the pan and place in an ovenproof dish with a little of the syrup. Any leftover syrup can be saved and used for another recipe. It's great for poaching apples too, which you could serve warm, with the syrup and a spoon of good vanilla ice cream.

To make the crumble, blitz everything apart from the almonds in a food processor until crumbly, then stir in the almonds by hand. Or you can do it by hand – rubbing the butter into the flour, then stirring everything else in – which I prefer. Not that it tastes better, it's just a rather restful, vaguely meditative activity. Scatter this mixture over the pears, as much as you personally like – the rest can go in the freezer for next time. Bake the crumble for 20 minutes, or until golden brown. Serve with cream, ice cream or custard.

AUTUMN TEATIME

As the days start to get shorter, I often forego lunch in favour of trying to do as much as possible outside before it gets dark. So come afternoon, I have definitely earned a slice of something to go with that always welcome mug of tea.

Butternut Tea Loaf

This came about because I had a sorry-looking bit of butternut squash left over in the fridge. There was not enough for soup, but it wasn't sorry enough to give to Duffy and Delilah, our ancient, much-loved Kune Kune pigs, who do an excellent job of making sure we don't waste any vegetable scraps at all. The *River Cottage Veg* book has a recipe for a pumpkin tea bread which called for just about the amount of butternut I had left, but as I was missing some of the other ingredients it stipulated, I had to fiddle around with it a bit. I was quite pleased with the result, which is almost more savoury than sweet. You could butter it, but I'm not sure it needs it. But a big mug of tea, as always, is a must.

200g (7oz) dark or light
   muscovado sugar
4 eggs, separated
200g (7oz) butternut squash or
   pumpkin, grated
zest and juice of 1 unwaxed lemon
50g (1¾oz) pecan nuts, roughly
   chopped

100g (3½oz) raisins or sultanas
50g (1¾oz) ground almonds
50g (1¾oz) desiccated coconut, or
   more ground almonds
200g (7oz) self-raising flour
¼ teaspoon salt
1 teaspoon ground ginger
¼ teaspoon ground turmeric

Makes 1 loaf

Preheat your oven to 170°C (325°F), Gas Mark 3, and line a 900-g (2-lb) loaf tin. Using an electric whisk, whisk together the sugar and egg yolks until you have a smooth, pale coffee-coloured mixture. Add the butternut, lemon juice and zest, the pecans, dried fruit, ground almonds and desiccated coconut. Stir gently to combine well. Then add the self-raising flour, salt and spices and stir again.

In a clean bowl, with clean beaters, whisk the egg whites until they form soft peaks and add them, one large spoonful at a time, to the rest of the mixture, folding them in with a large metal spoon. When they are all combined, spoon the mixture into the loaf tin and put in the oven. Check it after 1 hour by sticking a skewer in it and seeing if it comes out clean. I found this loaf needed about 10 minutes more, but the skewer will tell you!

Once cooked, let the loaf cool in the tin for about 5 minutes and then on a wire rack. It is very good warm, if you don't have the patience to wait until it is completely cool...

Mum's Chocolate Biscuit Cake

Mum was not much of a baker when I was a child. She could make a good, if basic, Victoria sponge for a birthday (I liked mine flavoured with orange, my brother and dad chocolate, with a fudgy icing) but as someone who doesn't much eat cake, she wasn't going to spend much time and energy making them. And I have to admit I feel the same. But this no-cook cake was a childhood staple – no picnic would be without it. It is ridiculously easy and adaptable – so you can make it entirely to your taste. The only downside is it is almost impossible to eat only one piece.

250g (9oz) digestive biscuits, or a
  mix of digestives and ginger nuts
125g (4½oz) butter, plus extra for
  greasing

2 tablespoons golden syrup
1 heaped tablespoon good-quality
  cocoa
icing sugar, for dusting

Serves 6

You can put the biscuits in a food processor and pulse until they are broken up – you don't want them to be too small or too even. Which is why it is better (and a lot more fun) to put them in a bag and bash them with a rolling pin.

Melt the butter, golden syrup and cocoa together in a medium pan then stir in the broken biscuits. Turn out into a greased, loose-bottomed tin (I use a 22-cm/8½-in square tin), spread it out evenly and press it down. Chill in the fridge until solid. Remove from the tin, dust with icing sugar and cut into chunks.

This is the basic version, but you can stir in other ingredients along with the biscuits. My favourite: zest and juice of 1 unwaxed orange, a handful of roughly chopped pecan nuts, chopped dried apricots and 3 balls of stem ginger, chopped. Or try halved Maraschino cherries, sultanas and roughly chopped almonds.

SOME AUTUMN EXTRAS

We have come to the time of year when every now and then you need a warm drink that isn't tea.

Mulled Cider

Glühwein, that warm, spicy red wine that has become a ubiquitous winter warmer, is, I think, entirely eclipsed by this version made with cider. You don't get that slightly roof-of-the-mouth dryness you can experience when drinking not-terribly-nice red wine, which the spices often do little to disguise. By contrast, the fruity appleyness of the cider is the perfect foil for the spices and will warm you to the core.

juice of 6 clementines

1.5 litres (2¾ pints) cider

2 cinnamon sticks

1 bay leaf

1 star anise

3 cloves

1 teaspoon allspice berries

2 teaspoons brown sugar (or more)

a splash or 2 of orange liqueur or
  Armagnac

Serves 4

Put the clementine juice and cider in a saucepan. Add all the other ingredients to the pan and simmer gently for around 20 minutes. Then ladle into mugs or heatproof glasses.

Damson Gin

I have a Kilner jar of damson gin in the making in my kitchen at the moment. Once a week I turn it, shaking the dark fruit and the remnants of the sugar from the bottom of the jar, and have a little taste. Just to check it is doing what it should. In another week or so it will be ready to strain and put into bottles. Then, in an exercise of extreme restraint, I have to leave it – hidden away in a cool, dark place – for at least three months, ideally longer, while the full, fruity warmth of the damsons' flavour develops. Luckily, I have some damson gin I made last year, so I don't have to wait before I can make what is, I think, the perfect autumn cocktail (see page 216).

450g (1lb) damsons, washed and
   pricked with the point of a knife

225g (8oz) sugar
600ml (20fl oz) gin

Makes about 1 litre (1¾ pints)

Put the damsons in a large Kilner jar. Tip in the sugar and then pour in the gin. Seal the top and give it a good shake to mix everything up. Over the next week, shake it every day so the sugar doesn't just settle at the bottom. And then for the next 8–10 weeks, tip it upside down once a week, watching the gin take on the jewel-like colour of the fruit.

Now it is ready to strain and seal into bottles and be left quietly in the dark for 3 months to do its magic. It is delicious sipped, neat, from a small glass, but mixed with mulled apple juice it is sensational.

My Favourite Cocktail
for Autumn

750ml (1⅜ pints) freshly pressed
   apple juice
1 cinnamon stick
4 cloves

1 star anise
1 unwaxed orange
4 shots of Damson Gin

Serves 4

Pour the apple juice into a saucepan and add the spices and 2 thick strips of orange rind removed with a vegetable peeler. Bring to the boil, then simmer gently for 5 minutes.

Pour a shot of damson gin into 4 mugs or Duralex glasses. Pour over the spiced apple juice, straining it through a tea strainer. Decorate with halved slices of orange.

WINTER

Winter is for wrapping up, hunkering down, nurturing. Although I will bemoan the short hours of daylight, the mud, the chapped hands and permanent drip on the end of my nose (something that seems unstoppable when you reach middle age), there are lots of things I enjoy about this time of year. Frosty mornings, the childlike excitement when it snows, the call of tawny owls, the cathedral-like grandeur of the woods. That wonderful, luxurious relief of coming in from the cold.

There's lots of farm work to do. The cattle and pigs and goats are in their sheds, bedded down in warm straw, and the twice-daily ritual of checking water, mucking out and feeding, although time-consuming is, for me, a comforting start and end to a day. Animals are always pleased to see you, particularly if you're carrying a bucket of feed! And if it is one of those wet, cheerless mornings when the sun never seems to bother to rise, pigs, especially, have an unerring ability to perk you up. An early morning cuddle with a pig and suddenly all seems well in the world. The sheep, protected by their woolly fleeces and thick hedges to hide behind, stay outside until they are due to lamb. We take hay and feed out to them, as there's not much in the way of grass. They'll be scanned in December, so we'll know how many lambs to expect and when lambing time comes it is always greeted with an excited anticipation. It is hard work, and you don't get much sleep, but witnessing new life entering the world always feels miraculous and optimistic.

I like the sociability of winter – small gatherings in the kitchen, wine and chat and laughter, the curtains drawn, hiding us from the weather and the dark. And food, of course, is important. I want food that is bolstering and comforting, yes, but I don't want bland stodge. I want strong flavours, food that is reminiscent of warmer days and happy times. Oh, and lots and lots of tea.

A Soda Bread for Winter
with Oats & Black Treacle

I have a special fondness for this recipe. It was given to me by my friend, Jennifer, the wonderful founder of Dough & Daughters. Despite my protestations, she said even I could make this bread and she was right! Inspired by her Scandinavian roots, it is a beautiful, rich, dark bread – perfect alongside stews, with a hunk of cheese, with smoked fish, or just on its own with a slathering of salty butter.

400g (14oz) self-raising flour, plus
   extra for dusting
50g (1¾oz) oats
1 teaspoon bicarbonate of soda
3 generous tablespoons black treacle

200ml (7fl oz) buttermilk, or
   100ml (3½fl oz) milk mixed with
   100ml (3½fl oz) natural yogurt
oil for greasing

Makes 1 loaf

Preheat your oven to 180°C (350°F), Gas Mark 4. Put the flour, oats and bicarbonate of soda into a large bowl. In a measuring jug, mix the buttermilk or milk/yogurt mixture with the treacle. A good tip here is to dip your treacle measuring spoon into a cup of boiling water between scoops, so your treacle will just slide off and not stick. Top the combined liquids up to 300ml (½ pint) with water and stir well.

Tip the liquids into the bowl of dry ingredients and mix gently until they are all combined. Tip the dough out onto a lightly floured surface and shape it into a flattish round loaf – it will look (I'm afraid to say) a bit like a cow pat, but that's what you want. Place it on an oiled baking tray and cut a deep cross in the top with a knife. Bake for 25–30 minutes. Tap the bottom and if it sounds hollow, it is ready. Cool on a wire rack while, in my case, looking at it with amazed pride!

BREAKFASTS FOR WINTER

꘎

Breakfast, it is so often claimed, is the meal that sets you up for the day. So I want food that feels a little bit celebratory, flavours and textures that are considered and indulgent. The food equivalent of a beautiful thick, soft, woollen blanket.

Spiced Dried Fruit Compote

This is another of Mum's stalwarts. I'm sure I remember she gave me this for breakfast when I stayed with her one winter, but I've just read her recipe and it is full of booze. Probably why it was so memorable. Oh well…the alcohol has probably boiled off by the time you come to eat it. I quote directly, 'Glass of red wine, port or brandy or mix it up a bit, so a small glass of red wine and a splash of brandy goes well.' So essentially, Mum was giving me a cocktail for breakfast. However, when I tried it, it did, as Mum claimed, go very well.

But if you feel that fruit cooked in red wine and brandy perhaps isn't the most responsible start to a day, you can eat it later (Mum says it's great with ginger ice cream and crunchy almond biscuits). Or cook the fruit in a mixture of orange and cranberry juice which works very well too – I made a version using the juice of two oranges (rather than just one) and 200ml (7fl oz) of cranberry juice.

250g (9oz) dried apricots

250g (9oz) dried figs (the soft ones), cut in half and stalks removed

250g (9oz) pitted prunes

1 unwaxed orange, plus the juice of another

2 balls of preserved ginger in syrup

1 cinnamon stick

200ml (7fl oz) red wine or cranberry juice

a glug of brandy or port (a tablespoon, I would say, optional)

Serves 8

Put all the dried fruit into a saucepan. Slice the whole orange, cut each slice in half and add to the pan with the orange juice. Chop the preserved ginger into small pieces and add to the pan with the cinnamon stick and the wine or cranberry juice and the brandy or port, if using, and top up with water so the fruit is just covered.

Simmer for about 20–30 minutes until the fruit is soft but not disintegrating.

Leave to cool a bit in its juice, then serve, nicely warm, with thick Greek yogurt or your own Homemade Yogurt (see page 231). It will keep for a week in the fridge.

Seville Orange Marmalade

Ludo's dad was an inveterate marmalade-maker and Ludo, who doesn't spend a great deal of time in the kitchen, has nonetheless carried on the family tradition to become the new Chief of Marmalade. Come early January, when Seville oranges reach the shops, Ludo gets positively twitchy until he has laid in a hoard of this thick-skinned fruit. Some will be instantly turned into marmalade – the kitchen transforming into a wizard's den of bubbling cauldrons and fragrant steam – and others will be stashed away, whole, in the freezer for when their short season is over.

Ludo likes his marmalade to retain that bitter sweetness that is unique to Seville oranges and will try to get away with using less sugar than stipulated – which, by law (and I'm not joking), means that what he is making is not strictly marmalade. So the recipe here is from Angharad, our dear friend, neighbour and unrivalled queen of preserves. If you can't quite summon the will to make your own marmalade, you can still eat hers by buying it online on The Preservation Society website.

1.2 litres (2 pints) water

juice of ½ lemon

500g (1lb 2oz) Seville oranges

1kg (2lb 4oz) sugar

Makes 5–7 jars

Put the water in a large pan on the hob and bring to the boil. In the meantime, scrub the oranges and, once the water is boiling, drop them into the pan, whole and just as they are. Boil them for about 2½ hours, until they are completely soft and can be pierced with a knife. Leave them in the water to cool.

In the meantime, prepare your jars. Although this recipe will make 5–7 jars, it is always worth sterilizing more jars than you need because nothing is more annoying that not having enough jars ready when you want to fill them. Wash your jars with warm soapy water, rinse but don't dry them. Instead arrange them on a baking tray and put them in a preheated oven at 140°C (275°F), Gas Mark 1, and there they can sit until you need them. Wash the lids and leave in a bowl of boiling water.

Put a saucer in your freezer (this is so you can test your setting point later).

Once your oranges have cooled enough to handle, take them out and measure the remaining cooking water. You'll need 850ml (1½ pints). If you have less, just top it up with more water. Return the cooking water to the pan. Cut the oranges in half, removing the pips with a fork over a bowl. Strain any juice from the pips into your reserved cooking water and discard the pips.

Cut the cooked oranges into shreds – as thick as you like them to be – and put them and the lemon juice in the cooking water, bring to the boil, cook for 5 minutes and then add the sugar. Stir to dissolve the sugar, then bring back to the boil. Keep the mixture at a rolling boil (if you have a thermometer it needs to be 105°C/221°F) for 10–15 minutes until the setting point is reached.

Test to see if it has reached the setting point by dropping a bit of the marmalade onto your cold saucer. If it remains runny, you will need to keep the mixture boiling a bit longer, but if it starts to set, take the pan off the boil and leave to cool for 10 minutes before transferring the marmalade to the jars and sealing them with their lids.

Bacon & Marmalade Sandwich

Ludo is horrified that I am admitting to this 'abomination' of a breakfast. And slightly put out that I would use his marmalade in such a way. But unlikely (or disgusting) as it sounds, bacon together with sharp, bitter marmalade between two slices of bread (or toast, but I prefer bread) is a very fine way to start a day. You want crispy bacon, smoky and perhaps a tiny bit burned at the edges.

2–3 rashers of smoked streaky
  bacon
2 slices of bread (or a roll)

butter
Seville orange marmalade

Serves 1
Fry your bacon in a dry pan until crisp. Toast your bread if you prefer your sandwich toasted. Butter the bread or toast, spread one piece liberally with marmalade, top with the bacon rashers, then the second slice of bread and squash it with the flat of your hand just slightly, because somehow that makes it feel like a proper sandwich.

Granola

Shop-bought granolas, with their pretty packaging and enticing health claims, promise so much but are all too often bland, over-sweet and over-priced. As soon as I discovered how easy it is to make granola, how you can tailor it to include all the things you like best, I never bought the ready-made stuff again. And the crunch came – literally – when my friend Polly gave me a top tip that had been passed on to her which meant, she said, that she never had disappointingly uncrunchy granola again…

Think of the following as a sort of foundation for a granola which you can change, add to, adapt and play with at will, until you find your perfect morning mix. Store in a large Kilner jar or other airtight storage jar.

175g (6oz) large rolled oats
175g (6oz) spelt flakes
250g (9oz) mixed nuts
50g (1¾oz) mixed seeds
50g (1¾oz) coconut flakes or
   desiccated coconut
½–1 teaspoon sea salt flakes

1 teaspoon ground cinnamon,
   ginger, cardamom or mixed
   spice
40g (1½oz) coconut oil
160g (5¾oz) maple syrup
1 egg white (Polly's top tip!)

Makes enough to fill a 1.8-litre (3¾-pint) jar

Preheat your oven to 200°C (400°F), Gas Mark 6, and line a large roasting tin with baking paper or one of those brilliant reusable nonstick baking mats. Put the oats and spelt flakes into a large bowl. Roughly chop the nuts and add them to the bowl along with the seeds, the coconut, the salt and spice.

Heat the coconut oil and maple syrup together in a small saucepan until the oil is melted and they are combined, then pour onto the dry ingredients and mix well. Whisk the egg white with a fork until it is slightly frothy and add to the mix. Give it all a good stir make sure everything is evenly coated. Tip it into the roasting tin, spread it out and put in the oven. Check it after about 10 minutes. If it has started to brown on top, give it a stir so the underside browns too. You just need to keep an eye on it. You will know how toasted you like it. Once it is browned to your idea of perfection, take it out of the oven and let it cool.

You will notice I have not added any dried fruit to this mix. If you want to, I would add it after cooking, once the mixture has cooled, otherwise I find the fruit goes rather hard and chewy and it seems to make the mixture soggier. Or just add a handful of dried fruit when you are going to eat it, then you can decide if it is a raisin kind of day, or apricot. I will sometimes add the zest of an unwaxed lemon or an orange before cooking, which just adds a nice citrus tang.

Granola with dried fruit

Eat on its own (it is a slightly addictive snack) or, more conventionally, with milk or – better – yogurt. Incidentally, as you are about to see, making yogurt is easier than you might think, and is a good way to cut down on waste plastic, so you can feel virtuous while you are making it.

How to Make Yogurt

To make yogurt, you will need a wide-necked Thermos flask or two, a thermometer, a saucepan and a Kilner jar or two for storing your yogurt in the fridge once made. You will also need 3 tablespoons of organic live yogurt (I know – you need yogurt to make yogurt, but once you've made it you can use your own to make the next batch) and 500ml (18fl oz) of milk. Goats' or cows' milk both work well, and you can use whole milk, semi-skimmed or skimmed. The less fat in the milk, the less thick the yogurt.

Let your live yogurt come up to room temperature before you start. When you are ready to make your batch of yogurt, put the milk in a saucepan and heat to 85°C (185°F), stirring occasionally so it doesn't catch on the bottom of the pan. Once it has reached that temperature, take it off the heat and allow to cool to 46°C (115°F). At this point, whisk the live yogurt into the milk and transfer the mixture to a warmed Thermos flask. Screw the lid on and leave it for 8 hours, by which time you will have yogurt. Leave it longer if you want it to be thicker and stronger tasting. Transfer to clean jars and store in the fridge for up to 3 days.

To your yogurt and granola breakfast, you can add fresh or frozen and defrosted fruit, or a compote. The Blackberry & Apple Compote on page 162 is good with it but in February, nothing is more cheering than the arrival of the first of the season's forced rhubarb.

Rhubarb Compote
for Breakfast & Beyond

Forced rhubarb sounds unkind, like something that should be boycotted on grounds of cruelty, but it is a growing technique that dates back to 1817. Yorkshire is famous for it – there is a 'rhubarb triangle' where, once the rhubarb roots are two years old, they are dug up and transplanted to sheds and left in the dark. Once Nature triggers them to start growing, their beautiful pink stems will start to shoot upwards, seeking light, which they won't find.

Unable to photosynthesize, the plants don't waste energy growing the huge characteristic leaves. As a result we get long, straight, sweet, tender pink stems of rhubarb at just the time of year when we are craving something fresh and pretty. I am, unashamedly, including rhubarb in recipes for every time of day – as a savoury main course (see page 60), as a pudding (see pages 63, 137, 139 and 265) and as a drink (see page 79), as well as for breakfast – because it is just too good not to make the most of.

If you buy rhubarb from the supermarket it tends to come in 400-g (14-oz) packets which will make enough compote for breakfast for about four people, but it keeps very well in a container in the fridge and you can use it in so many ways, it is often worth making more than you immediately need.

400g (14oz) rhubarb   sugar
zest of 1 unwaxed orange, juice of ½
 (optional)

Serves 4
You can poach the rhubarb in a pan on the hob or roast it – roasting tends to help it keep its shape better. If you are roasting it, preheat your oven to 200°C (400°F), Gas Mark 6. Trim the rhubarb and cut into 5-cm (2-in) lengths. Put it in a pan or a roasting tin with the orange juice and zest, if using, or a splash of water (the rhubarb releases lots of liquid as it cooks, so you only need add a little). Sprinkle on some sugar – this early rhubarb is much sweeter than the later, garden-grown varieties, so you might find you don't need much. Cook until the rhubarb softens but doesn't entirely lose its shape – usually around 6–8 minutes.

MAIN COURSES FOR WINTER

꒜

Unashamed and unabashed comfort food. Warm spices, fragrant steam – food that transports and delights and is, on occasion, a little bit escapist.

Lentil & Tomato Soup
with Cumin

This is my go-to hearty, comforting and filling winter soup. It is made – or can be – with almost entirely storecupboard ingredients and can be adapted or added to as you see fit. Don't like cumin? Use fennel seeds, or no seeds. You can add a carrot cut into batons, or cubes of sweet potato (put in at the same time as the lentils) to make it more veggie stew than soup.

I like stirring in a handful of spinach leaves if I have some, right at the end of cooking, so they just wilt, or a handful of fresh coriander and a squeeze of lime juice. Or top it with kale leaves, rubbed with olive oil, sprinkled with salt and crisped up in a hot oven for 5 minutes or so. Or put the soup just as it is in a flask and take it to sustain you on a big winter walk.

a glug of olive or rapeseed oil

1 onion, finely chopped

1 garlic clove, grated (use one of those super-fine graters you might use for zesting) or finely chopped

1 thumb-sized piece of ginger, peeled and grated

1 tablespoon cumin seeds

1 tablespoon garam masala

250g (9oz) dried red lentils

1 litre (1¾ pints) vegetable stock (fresh or from a cube)

500g (1lb 2oz) passata

160ml (5½oz) can coconut cream

salt and pepper

Serves 4

Heat the oil in a large saucepan over a medium heat. Add the onion with a good pinch of salt and sweat for 5 minutes until it starts to soften and turn translucent. Add the garlic and ginger and stir. Continue to cook for another 5 minutes or so until everything is soft and fragrant.

Add the spices and stir into the onion mixture until they are well mixed and the lovely spicy smell starts to drift up from the pan. Add the lentils and stir them around until they are well incorporated with the spices and onion. Add the stock, passata and coconut cream, stir and cook on a gentle heat for 20–25 minutes, stirring every now and then, until the lentils are soft. Taste. Season. Eat. Purr.

Ludo's Cheese on Toast

Ludo has a small cooking repertoire, but what he cooks is seriously good. Cheese on toast as far as I was concerned was exactly that: a piece of toast topped with slices of cheese and put under the grill until it melted. Which is fine, in a not-very-exciting way. But when Ludo made me his version of cheese on toast, I realized that this was the man I wanted to marry. I asked him to write the recipe, so this is how he makes it, verbatim. Although I will suggest, because he forgot, to preheat your grill. If you want someone to marry you, try it!

Grate a good amount of cheese (Red Leicester is my favourite) into a mixing bowl – enough for two slices of toast (about 150g/5½oz of cheese). Add a raw egg, a few healthy glugs of Worcestershire sauce, season with salt and pepper and mix it all really well to produce a gooey cheesy mush.

Under a grill, on a tray, toast ONE SIDE of your bread – wholemeal with seeds is nice. When the one side is nicely toasted, remove the grill pan, turn the bread over and carefully butter around the edges of the untoasted side – this should stop the edges burning when you grill the cheesy mix. Dollop the cheese mix evenly across the untoasted side of the bread and spread as close to the edges as you can. Put it back under the grill and keep a close eye on it as it cooks. You want the cheese to be nicely melted throughout, and the top to be just starting to form a few black spots. Out it comes, straight onto a plate. Delicious with a tomato (or even Tommy K) on the side, but best with a good squirt of sharp English mustard.

Slow-roasted Shoulder of Goat
with Pomegranate Slaw & Harissa Yogurt

Goat meat is not widely eaten in the UK. I'm not sure why this should be – perhaps because lamb is always widely available. If you find it on a menu at all, it is usually as a curry, and although I am never one to dismiss a curry, it can be eaten in many other ways. Don't imagine that it will have the same distinctive taste as goats' cheese, because it doesn't. It is soft, full of flavour and not so very different from lamb. It is a very lean meat, so it needs cooking at low temperatures for a long time, and it is also very low in cholesterol (lower than chicken) so it's healthy too.

This recipe is one I often do on Christmas Day, partly because I'm just not a fan of 'turkey and all the trimmings' and mainly because we have a tradition of going to the beach for the day. Before we set off, I put this in the oven at a really low temperature (around 140°C/275°F/Gas Mark 1) and cover the tin in foil. When we get back around eight hours later, I'll turn the oven up to about 160°C (325°F), Gas Mark 3, take off the foil and let it cook for another hour or so. This dish is wonderfully low-maintenance and still feels special and festive. The cooking temperature in the recipe overleaf is for when you want it ready to serve in 3–4 hours.

Slow-roasted Shoulder of Goat

1 bone-in kid shoulder, about 1.5kg
  (3lb 5oz)

red wine (optional)

2 teaspoons ground cumin

2 teaspoons ground coriander

1 teaspoon ground cinnamon

3 teaspoons sumac

zest of 1 unwaxed lemon

1 tablespoons rose harissa

olive oil

salt and pepper

Serves 4–8, depending on what else you're serving it with

Preheat the oven to 160°C (325°F), Gas Mark 3. Put the goat shoulder into a roasting tin lined with baking paper. Pour 1cm (½in) of red wine (if using) or water into the bottom of the tin. Slash the meat in a few places then season well with salt.

Mix together the spices, lemon zest, harissa, a pinch of pepper and enough olive oil to bring it to a paste consistency. Spread this all over the top of the goat shoulder. You can either cook it straight away or leave it to marinate in the fridge overnight.

Put the goat shoulder into the preheated oven and cook for 3½–4 hours, basting it every now and then. The meat is ready once it is falling off the bone and can be flaked with a fork. If at any point it looks like it's drying out, add a little more wine or water to the bottom of the tray and cover the roasting tin with foil. When it's ready, take it out of the oven, cover loosely with foil and let it rest for about 10 minutes before flaking it with a fork and serving.

For my Christmas version, I might serve this with roasted beetroots and couscous with lots of chopped herbs, with a dollop of the Harissa Yogurt on page 240 on the side, but this dish is also really good served with flatbreads and

a Middle Eastern-inspired Slaw, as shown in the photograph on page 239. This jewel-coloured pomegranate slaw is also really good alongside grilled halloumi.

Pomegranate Slaw
with Harissa Yogurt

2 handfuls of young kale or baby kale, stalks removed, leaves chopped

1 tablespoon olive oil

2 large carrots, peeled

½ small red cabbage, finely shredded

2 spring onions, finely chopped

a small bunch of parsley, chopped

leaves from a small bunch of mint, finely chopped

1 tablespoon sumac

100g (3½oz) pomegranate seeds

FOR THE DRESSING

juice of ½ lemon

6 tablespoons olive oil

1 small garlic clove, grated

2 tablespoons pomegranate molasses

salt and pepper

Serves 4–8, depending on what else you're serving it with
Put the kale into a large bowl and add the tablespoon of oil and a pinch of salt. Massage and scrunch the oil and salt into the kale, using your hands to soften it so that it wilts. Using a vegetable peeler, peel ribbons of carrot into the bowl with the kale. Add the cabbage, spring onions and herbs and mix well.

Whisk together the ingredients for the dressing. Taste and adjust the seasoning if it needs it. Pour the dressing over the vegetables along with the sumac and mix really well. Scatter over the pomegranate seeds and leave to one side until ready to serve.

FOR THE HARISSA YOGURT

1–2 tablespoons rose harissa

250ml (9fl oz) full-fat natural
yogurt

Mix the harissa into the yogurt. Voilà!

Pig Cheeks in Sherry

Our friend Graham, the charcutier – he who taught me how to cure bacon – also introduced us to the culinary joy that is a slow-cooked pig's cheek. It was not something I had ever eaten, or was even aware was something you could buy. But with the so-called unfashionable cuts of meat becoming fashionable, these meltingly tender and tasty bits of pork are easier to find. Graham braised his in cider with carrots, onions, bay and thyme. I've since experimented, and love this Spanish-inspired version, braised in sherry. I eat it with a hunk of crusty bread and a salad of peppery leaves.

600g (1lb 5oz) pig cheeks
1 tablespoon plain flour, seasoned
   with salt and pepper
oil
2 onions, finely chopped
2 garlic cloves, finely sliced
1 tablespoon smoked paprika
1 tablespoon ground cumin

250ml (9fl oz) dry sherry
750ml (1⅜ pint) chicken or beef
   stock (fresh or from a cube)
a small bunch of flat leaf parsley,
   chopped
a handful of toasted flaked
   almonds
salt and pepper

Serves 4

Preheat your oven to 150°C (300°F), Gas Mark 2. Toss the pig cheeks in the seasoned flour to coat. Heat a glug of oil in a heavy-based casserole dish and brown the cheeks on both sides (you may have to do this in batches), then set aside on a plate. Add a little more oil to the casserole, if needed, then add the onions and a pinch of salt, and cook over a medium heat until they are soft and translucent. Add the garlic and cook for a minute or 2, until it releases its aroma.

Put the pig cheeks (and any juices) back in the pot and sprinkle with the smoked paprika and cumin. Pour in the sherry and let it bubble for a moment, before adding the stock. Scrape to release any bits stuck to the pan. Bring to the boil, then cover and transfer to the oven. Cook for 2–3 hours until the cheeks are meltingly soft.

Check the seasoning, sprinkle with chopped parsley and toasted flaked almonds and serve with mash, or, perhaps more in keeping, patatas bravas. Eat while listening to Rodrigo's *Concierto de Aranjuez*, for the full experience.

Spinach & Feta Parcels
with Sambal Hijau

When Ben was in his early twenties he took off on a big trip around Asia. His budget was tight, so most of the time he stayed with families who had a room to rent out to travellers. As someone who had always enjoyed spicy food and thought chillies were only worth eating if they blew your head off, the food he ate and then learned to cook in the homes he stayed in gave him a whole new appreciation of spices and flavours. So much so, that when he returned to the UK, he set up a business (Parva Spices) making sambals (which are relishes used in an almost infinite number of ways) and an amazing array of spice mixes and sauces. You can buy them online but we don't have to because he lives just

down the hill! I spent a very happy afternoon in his kitchen learning how to make sambal hijau, and then using it to add an aromatic, herby kick to his dangerously moreish spinach and feta parcels.

There are not many things this sambal won't go with. It's lovely with scrambled eggs or as a relish with goats' cheese. Ben spreads it on fish fillets before grilling them. It would go very well with lamb chops, or roast chicken.

FOR THE SAMBAL HIJAU

130g (4¾oz) green chillies, stalks removed, roughly chopped

50g (1¾oz) garlic

55g (2oz) ginger, chopped (but don't bother to peel it)

25g (1oz) mint, roughly chopped

25g (1oz) fresh coriander, roughly chopped

30g (generous 1oz) brown sugar

10g (¼oz) sea salt flakes

2 tablespoons vegetable oil

125ml (4fl oz) rice vinegar

Makes 3 jars

Put all the ingredients in the bowl of a food processor and pulse until everything is well chopped and combined. You will have a thick, almost pesto-like texture. Spoon the sambal into sterilized jars (see page 226). Once opened, keep in the fridge and use within a week.

FOR THE PARCELS

a knob of butter

a good pinch of freshly grated nutmeg

300g (10½oz) spinach, rinsed

2 eggs

100g (3½oz) feta cheese, crumbled

20g (¾oz) pine nuts

1–2 tablespoon Sambal Hijau

1 pack of ready-rolled puff pastry

salt and pepper

Serves 4

Preheat your oven to 220°C (425°F), Gas Mark 7, and line a baking tray with baking paper. Melt the butter in a large saucepan and add the nutmeg. Add the damp spinach to the saucepan and stir for 3–4 minutes until wilted. Allow to cool. Once cooled, squeeze out all the water from the spinach – Ben's trick is to put it between 2 clean tea towels and roll it with a rolling pin. Then finely chop it.

In a large bowl, beat 1 of the eggs lightly, then add the spinach, the feta and pine nuts. Add 1–2 tablespoons of sambal (to taste), season with salt and pepper and stir until everything is well mixed.

Beat the remaining egg in a small bowl. Divide the pastry into quarters, roughly square in shape. Divide the filling between the 4 squares of pastry and brush the edges with beaten egg. Fold the pastry over on the diagonal to form a triangle and use the prongs of a fork to press the edges together. Put your parcels on the baking tray, brush with the remaining egg and bake for 20–25 minutes until puffed and golden. Allow to cool for a few minutes on a wire rack and then eat. Or you can eat them cold.

Sausages in Red Wine

Sometimes circumstances call for food that is simple, reliable and satisfying to eat. This is all of those things. I've been cooking it for years and it never fails.

Almost two decades ago we were travelling around southern Africa, living out of a battered old pick-up truck. After a particularly rough two weeks or so wild camping in Mozambique, we crossed the border into Swaziland. We found a campsite that had showers (oh the bliss) and in the small town bought a cast iron cooking pot on three legs, known locally as a *potjie*, and some meaty sausages called *boerewors*. We cooked over a fire, ate straight from the pot and had leftovers for breakfast the next day. Life was good.

oil

8 good-quality sausages

150g (5½oz) pancetta, cut into
   cubes

2 red onions, cut into wedges

250g (9oz) chestnut mushrooms,
   cut in quarters

2 garlic cloves, sliced

2 heaped teaspoons plain flour

1 teaspoon mustard powder

300ml (½ pint) red wine

200ml (7fl oz) stock (fresh or from
   a cube)

2–3 sprigs of thyme or 1 teaspoon
   dried thyme

1–2 bay leaves

a handful of roughly chopped
   parsley

salt and pepper

Serves 4

Heat a glug of oil in a large casserole over a medium–high heat and brown the
sausages. Remove and set aside. Add the pancetta, onions and mushrooms
to the same pan (you probably won't need to add any more oil) and fry until
softened and slightly browned on the edges.

Add the garlic and after a minute or 2, sprinkle over the flour and mustard
powder. Stir well for about a minute then add the red wine and stock. Stir so
the flour is absorbed into the wine, then return the sausages to the pan with the
thyme and bay leaves. Season with salt and pepper, put the lid on the casserole
and leave to simmer over a low–medium heat for about 30 minutes.

Take the lid off and cook for another 15–20 minutes, to let the winey juices
reduce to form a rich gravy. Check to see if it needs more seasoning, sprinkle
liberally with roughly chopped parsley and eat. Mash is the obvious thing to
go with this: good old potato mash, or a mixture of potato and celeriac. Or go
slightly rogue and have mashed butternut or sweet potato.

Roasted Fish
with Parma Ham & Pea Purée

I've probably cooked this for just about everyone I know. It requires almost no preparation, cooks quickly, looks mildly impressive on the plate and leaves practically no washing up. And it has a good mix of textures that somehow make what is a very simple dish seem almost sophisticated. Well, as far as I do sophistication anyway. Although this recipe is for two, it is easy to cook for one or to scale up for as many as you like.

oil

2 fillets of skinless fish (salmon, cod or haddock)

4 slices of Parma ham or speck

chilli flakes (optional)

400g (14oz) frozen peas

a dollop of crème fraîche

2 roasted garlic cloves (shop-bought or homemade – see page 77)

a handful of chopped chives

salt and pepper

lemon wedges, to serve

Serves 2

Preheat your oven to 220°C (425°F), Gas Mark 7. Pour a little bit of oil onto a nonstick baking tray and wipe with kitchen paper.

Check your fish fillets for pin bones, then wrap each fillet in 2 slices of ham, leaving the ends of each fillet exposed. Place on the baking sheet, drizzle over a little oil and season with salt, pepper and chilli flakes if you like them. Put in the oven for about 8–10 minutes – the cooking time will slightly depend on the size and thickness of the fillets, but you want the ham to have crisped up.

In the meantime, put the frozen peas in a pan, pour over boiling water, bring to the boil and cook for 3–4 minutes until they are soft. Drain, add the crème

fraîche and roasted garlic cloves and season with salt and pepper. Blitz with a hand blender until you have a not-too-smooth purée. Stir in the chopped chives, reserving some for garnish. Keep warm until the fish is ready (but it should be at more or less the same time).

Divide the pea purée between 2 plates. Top with the ham-wrapped fish fillets, sprinkle with the remaining chives and pop a wedge of lemon alongside.

Lamb Cawl
The Ultimate Welsh Winter Warmer

This is a classic Welsh dish that is somewhere between a soup and a stew. It can be made with beef or just vegetables as well as lamb and I love it. Like so many classic dishes, everyone has their way of doing it, often passed down the generations, and some are better than others. This is Penny's recipe, which came from her grandmother, who lived on Anglesey. It is a culinary duvet – warming and comforting. It is traditionally served with bread and cheese. You could always have a bit of green salad with it too.

2 tablespoons olive oil or lamb fat

500g (1lb 2oz) lamb neck fillet, sliced into 1-cm (½-in) slices

200g (7oz) parsnips, peeled and chopped

200g (7oz) carrots, peeled and chopped

250g (9oz) swede, peeled and chopped

250g (9oz) potatoes, peeled and chopped

500ml (18fl oz) lamb stock (fresh or from a cube)

1 teaspoon salt

a good bunch of parsley, chopped

1 sprig of rosemary

3 leeks, chopped

freshly ground black pepper

Serves 4–6

Preheat the oven to 170°C (325°F), Gas Mark 3.

A cast iron casserole would be ideal for this dish, but any large pan with a well-fitting lid that can go in the oven is fine. Heat the oil or lamb fat over a medium–high heat and seal the meat until golden. Add all the peeled and chopped vegetables to the pan, bar the leeks.

Cover with the lamb stock and add the seasoning, three-quarters of the parsley and the sprig of rosemary. Bring up to the boil, give everything a good stir, then put the casserole in the oven with the lid on. Forget about it for an hour, then remove any excess fat from the surface, check the seasoning and add the leeks. Leeks, like onions, dilute the effect of salt so make sure to season well. Place the casserole back in the oven for 20–30 minutes, until the meat and leeks are tender.

Serve in a soup bowl sprinkled with the remaining parsley and accompanied by plenty of crusty bread, Welsh cheese and a green salad. Like any stew, Welsh cawl is even better the day after you make it.

Prawn & Spinach Curry

A quick bowl of curry is sometimes just what a chilly winter weeknight demands, eaten without ceremony, but with appreciation, in front of the telly. If you like curry as much as I do, you will know that feeling you get when you've overindulged. I call it a curry hangover. But this prawn and spinach curry is light, fresh and perky – still satisfying and warming, but it doesn't leave you with that rather unpleasant sensation of being overstuffed. I like to serve it with brown rice (those pre-cooked microwaveable packets are very handy…) and a generous dollop of lime pickle or Ben's amazing Sambal Hijau (see page 244).

rapeseed oil

1 onion, sliced finely into half
  moons

2 garlic cloves, sliced

1 large thumb-sized piece of
  ginger, peeled and grated

1 tablespoon ground coriander

1 tablespoon ground cumin

½ teaspoon ground turmeric

200ml (7fl oz) coconut milk

125ml (4fl oz) vegetable stock
  (fresh or from a cube)

600g (1lb 5oz) raw prawns

zest and juice of 1 unwaxed lime,
  plus extra to serve

250g (9oz) baby spinach

a small bunch of fresh coriander,
  chopped

salt and pepper

lime wedges, to serve

Serves 4

Heat a glug of oil in a large saucepan over a medium heat. Add the onion, garlic and ginger and cook for 4–5 minutes until soft. Then add the spices, stir them in well and cook for a further minute. Pour in the coconut milk and the vegetable stock, bring to the boil and simmer for 2–3 minutes.

Add the prawns, lime juice and zest and simmer until the prawns are pink. Pile the spinach leaves in and pop a lid on for a minute or so until they have wilted down into the curry. Season, stir and then add some of the chopped coriander, reserving some to garnish.

Spoon over brown rice, scatter with the remaining coriander, squeeze over a bit more lime juice, grab a fork and settle down on the sofa for a quiet night in.

My Birthday Present

Mr Brock's Poached Pear in Mulled Cider Sorbet

✦

My birthday is in December, just a few days before Christmas and clashes with every office party, panto and carol service in the land. And I don't like parties anyway, so I never do much in the way of marking the occasion. However, when I turned 50, Freddie's mum and dad gave me the best birthday present ever: dinner at their house with a small gathering of my dearest friends.

As all the Morlands are very fine cooks, the food was amazing, but that evening Mr Brock surpassed himself. He created a sorbet using my favourite drink – cider – and mulling it to give it that wonderful, warming, winter flavour. He poached pears (another thing I love) in the cider and then turned the whole lot into the most glorious sorbet that was served alongside a delicious, buttery, crumbly pear tart. It was the perfect end to a perfect evening.

5 firm pears, peeled

1 cinnamon stick

2 star anise

2 cloves

2 cardamom pods, gently crushed

zest and juice of 1 unwaxed lemon

juice of 1 orange

750ml (1⅜ pint) cider

4 tablespoons caster sugar

generous grating of nutmeg

½ teaspoon vanilla extract

Serves 8–10

Put the pears in a pan big enough to hold them in one layer, add the rest of the ingredients and simmer until the pears are soft but not collapsing.

Remove the pears with a slotted spoon and core them before blending to form a thick, smooth purée. Sieve the liquid to remove the spices, boil furiously to reduce the volume by half, and then stir in the pear purée and chill.

Churn in an ice cream-maker until softly frozen, transfer to a tub or pot and put in the freezer. Again, take it out and put in the fridge for about 30 minutes before you want to eat it.

PUDDINGS FOR WINTER

Childhood favourites rub shoulders here with mildly more sophisticated – but still very simple – ideas to end a winter meal.

Baked Stuffed Apples

I do love a baked apple. They will be forever linked in my mind with shepherd's pie and Saturday lunchtimes, sitting around the table with my family – Mum, Dad in his 'weekend jumper', my brother hiding his peas under his fork. I loved (and still love) peeling away the wrinkled skin of the apple to reveal the steaming, fluffy interior with its core of spiced dried fruit. I could never wait until it was cool enough to eat, so would always burn my tongue.

Mum would stuff the cored apples with mincemeat, which is still one of my favourite ways to cook them (and super-easy) but I tried this combination as a bit of an experiment one day because I had some dried cranberries loitering in the cupboard which felt like they needed a purpose. I like it, but if you haven't got a packet of cranberries lurking in your kitchen, have fun experimenting with other types of dried fruit.

If you can make the stuffing a little in advance of cooking the apples, so much the better, as it will let the fruit plump up a bit, but it is not the end of the world if you don't.

50g (1¾oz) dried cranberries

50g (1¾oz) dried apricots,
  chopped

2 balls of stem ginger, finely
  chopped, plus 1 tablespoon of
  the syrup

zest of 1 unwaxed orange, juice of ½

a glug of brandy (optional)

runny honey

4 even-sized Bramley apples

20g (¾oz) butter

toasted flaked almonds, to serve

Serves 4

Preheat your oven to 180°C (350°F), Gas Mark 4. Put the cranberries, apricots and stem ginger into a bowl, add the stem ginger syrup, orange zest and juice and a glug of brandy, if using. Check for sweetness and add honey to taste. Leave aside for 30 minutes or more if you can.

When you are ready to cook, score the skin of the apples right around the middle, remove the cores and cut a thin slice from the bottoms so they stand up. Stand them in a baking dish. Stuff the fruit mixture into the centre of the apples, pressing it down so they are well packed. Drizzle any remaining liquid over the stuffing of each apple. Put a small knob of butter on the top of each one and bake in the oven for 35–45 minutes (depending on size) until the apples are soft, basting occasionally. Serve scattered with toasted flaked almonds and something cool and creamy – yogurt, cream or ice cream.

Clementine Cake
with an Orange & Pomegranate Salad

A self-confessed tentative cake-maker, when I attempted this one for the first time – lured by the irresistible combination of orangey citrus and almonds – it turned out to be nigh-on perfect. Consequently, I love it and probably bake it more often than any other cake. There are many versions out there, but they all

forego flour for ground almonds and use oranges, clementines or tangerines that are cooked until soft and then puréed. The result is a dense, fragrant sponge that is equally happy eaten unadorned, or with cream. Raspberries go well, either whole or as a coulis, but I love it with this simple orange salad and will offer crème fraîche with a shake of cinnamon for those who want it. Use blood oranges for the salad if you can find them as they are so decorative and taste wonderful.

FOR THE CAKE

375g (13oz) – or as near as possible – clementines or tangerines

oil for greasing

6 eggs

225g (8oz) golden caster sugar

250g (9oz) ground almonds

1 heaped teaspoon baking powder

Serves 8

Boil the whole fruit (in their skins) in a pan of water for 1–2 hours until soft. Let them cool, cut in half and remove the pips. Purée the fruit halves – skins and all – in a food processor until smooth. Preheat your oven to 190°C (375°F), Gas Mark 5, and grease and line a 20-cm (8-in) springform tin.

Beat the eggs with a fork, then stir in the sugar, almonds and baking powder. Once well mixed, add the fruit purée and stir until the fruit is evenly distributed in the mix. Pour into the prepared tin and cook for 1 hour. Check with your trusty skewer that it is cooked through. If it gets a bit too brown before the end of the cooking time, loosely cover with foil. Let it cool in the tin on a wire rack.

FOR THE ORANGE SALAD

6 oranges

1 teaspoon orange blossom water

2 tablespoons pomegranate seeds

2 tablespoons toasted flaked almonds

some mint leaves, shredded

Peel the oranges carefully, making sure you remove all the pith, then slice them into discs about 5mm (¼in) thick. Arrange them in a dish. Sprinkle over the orange blossom water and the pomegranate seeds. Just before serving, add a scattering of toasted flaked almonds and shredded mint leaves.

Spiced Poached Fruit
with Brown Sugar Mascarpone & Biscotti

The recipe for this wonderful, slightly unusual combination of tastes has been passed round almost every household in our valley. I ate it at Polly's house and begged her for the recipe. She got it from her neighbour Louise who got it from another mutual friend. And I've passed it on to countless people. So now we all serve it to each other, but somehow we never seem to tire of it.

Spiced Fruit
with Brown Sugar Mascarpone

375ml (13fl oz) white dessert wine	3 pears, peeled, quartered and cored
1 cinnamon stick	3 clementines, peeled and halved
1 star anise	3 figs, cut into quarters
1 red chilli, halved lengthways	50g (1¾oz) pomegranate seeds
150ml (¼ pint) water	
1 tablespoon caster sugar	

FOR THE BROWN SUGAR MASCARPONE

100g (3½oz) mascarpone	100ml (3½fl oz) double cream
1½ tablespoons dark muscovado sugar	

Serves 6

In a bowl, mix the mascarpone and the sugar together, then pour in the cream and stir gently until you have a smooth, coffee-coloured mixture. Cover and chill in the fridge until needed.

Pour the wine into a large, heavy-based saucepan. Add the cinnamon, star anise, the chilli halves and the water. Bring to the boil then remove from the heat and let sit for 15 minutes for the flavours to infuse.

When it's had its infusion time, put the pan back on the hob and bring it back to the boil, then turn down to a gentle simmer. Add the sugar, the pears and the clementines. If there is not enough liquid to completely cover the fruit, top up with water. Simmer until the pears are almost tender – about 10 minutes – then remove from the heat.

Add the figs and the pomegranate seeds and let it sit, covered, for 5 minutes. Serve warm, passing around the bowl of brown sugar mascarpone and a plate of biscotti.

Biscotti

I confess that more often than not I will just buy ready-made biscotti, but my friend Sarah gave me this recipe for the ones she makes. Sarah is a photographer and was commissioned to take photographs of a new, swanky hotel in California. Where she also had to stay, poor love. The biscotti that were served alongside tiny, perfect cups of espresso were, she said, sublime. Despite her not inconsiderable charms, the chef was rather reluctant to hand over his secrets so Sarah came up with her own version. They certainly taste five star to me.

100g (3½oz) skin-on almonds,
  sliced
325g (11½oz) plain flour, plus
  extra for dusting
200g (7oz) caster sugar
1 teaspoon baking powder

½ teaspoon salt
2 large eggs
zest of 1 unwaxed lemon
zest of 1 unwaxed orange
85g (3oz) dried blueberries
icing sugar, for dusting

Makes 24

Preheat your oven to 200°C (425°F), Gas Mark 7. Toast the almonds in a dry pan so they take on a little colour, then set aside. Mix the flour, sugar, baking powder and salt together in a large bowl. Beat the eggs and pour into the flour mixture along with the lemon and orange zest.

Stir with a wooden spoon then knead with your hands until you have a soft dough. Tip the dough out onto a lightly floured surface, then knead in the toasted almonds and blueberries.

Divide the mixture in half, then shape each half into a log, about 5cm (2in) in diameter. Put the logs of dough on a baking tray lined with baking paper, giving them a bit of room to spread – which they will. Dust them with icing sugar and put in the oven to bake for 25 minutes until pale gold. Test with a skewer to make sure they are cooked through and remove from the oven. Turn the oven down to 150°C (300°F), Gas Mark 2, and let the logs cool a little.

Once the logs are cool enough to handle, cut them into approximately 2-cm (¾-in) slices and lay them flat on the lined baking tray. Bake for 15 minutes, turn them over and bake the other side for 15 minutes too. If they haven't quite firmed up, bake for a further 5 minutes on each side. Leave to cool. If you are not eating them straight away, they will keep in an airtight tin for 2–3 weeks.

Rhubarb Fool

Fruit fools are so often thick with cream which, I'm sorry to say, is not my thing. But even Ludo, who loves cream, agrees that using cream in a rhubarb fool swamps the delicate texture of the fruit. So this fool uses only yogurt and because of my obsession with ginger – which luckily goes so well with rhubarb – I have used ginger yogurt, but you don't have to. This is one of those perfect puddings that is blissfully quick and easy to make but looks and tastes glorious. I love it with brandy snaps and have included a recipe on page 267, but shop-bought biscuits like those ridiculously moreish, spicy Dutch ones called speculaas cookies would be every bit as delicious.

500g (1lb 2oz) rhubarb, chopped
    into 3-cm (1¼-in) chunks
50g (1¾oz) golden caster sugar
2 tablespoons water

2 balls of stem ginger, finely
    chopped or grated
450g (1lb) ginger, vanilla or plain
    Greek yogurt

Serves 4–6

Put the rhubarb and sugar into a large, wide pan with the water. Gently cook over a medium–low heat for about 10 minutes, or until the rhubarb is soft and starting to collapse. Pour the cooked rhubarb into a sieve set over a bowl to drain. Leave the rhubarb to cool completely, ideally until fridge-cold. Reserve the strained liquid. While the rhubarb gets completely cold, put the strained liquid back into the pan and heat over a medium–high heat until it is reduced and syrupy. Leave to cool.

Gently fold the rhubarb and two-thirds of the chopped stem ginger through the yogurt. It looks lovely if you keep it quite streaky, so don't mix too vigorously. Divide between serving glasses or bowls, drizzle over the rhubarb syrup, top with the remaining chopped stem ginger and serve immediately or keep, covered, in the fridge for up to 24 hours if needed. The fools go beautifully with brandy snaps which, if you want to feel ridiculously proud of yourself – as I always do when I make them – can be made following the recipe opposite.

Brandy Snaps

It is, once again, my grandmother Paddy who is responsible for my love of brandy snaps. She would fill the crisp, caramel rolls with cream, but I would eschew the cream and just eat them as they were, scattering shards. There is no tidy way to eat a brandy snap. Nor should there be.

50g (1¾oz) butter
50g (1¾oz) demerara sugar
50g (1¾oz) golden syrup
50g (1¾oz) plain flour, sieved
½ teaspoon ground ginger

½ teaspoon lemon juice
½ teaspoon brandy (optional)
flavourless oil such as sunflower for
  greasing

Makes 10–14

Preheat the oven to 180°C (350°F), Gas Mark 4, and line 1 or 2 baking trays with baking paper or nonstick silicone mats. It is worth investing in these if you haven't got any. They make baking so much easier!

Put the butter, sugar and golden syrup into a small pan and heat gently, stirring often, until the sugar has dissolved, the butter has melted and everything looks syrupy. Be careful not to let the mixture get too hot. You don't want it to bubble. Remove the pan from the heat and leave to cool for a couple of minutes. Then stir in the flour, ground ginger, lemon juice and brandy, if using. Mix well.

Depending on the size of your baking trays, you will probably need to work in batches for the next stage. Dollop 1 heaped teaspoon of mixture onto the first tray, then add another spoonful 10cm (4in) away and so on, until you have 3 or 4 piles of mixture. Repeat with the other tray. Place in the oven and bake for about 10–12 minutes or until the mixture has spread, is dark golden and has little holes.

Meanwhile, oil the handle of a thick wooden spoon, metal whisk or similar. Remove the trays from the oven and leave to cool for 1–2 minutes. You need the mixture to be the right temperature so that it is firm enough to handle, but not so cool that you can't bend it. Once the mixture is the right temperature, scoop up each disc with a palette knife or fish slice and drape over the handle of your spoon or whisk and shape it into a tube. Leave to finish cooling on a wire rack.

Repeat with the remaining mixture. This will probably make 4 trays of brandy snaps. Once cool, they will store in an airtight container for a week.

WINTER TEATIME

Afternoon tea should be obligatory in winter. In fact, let's make it so! And let's honour this new tradition with no-nonsense, no-holds-barred bakes.

Chocolate & Marmalade Loaf

Not only is this possibly The Easiest Cake in the World to make, you can do the whole lot in one saucepan, so it produces almost no washing up either. Use best-quality dark chocolate. I like thick-cut Seville orange marmalade, but choose any marmalade you like. If it is a cold, wintery, slightly gloomy afternoon, this is the edible equivalent of thick socks and a roaring log fire…

125g (4½oz) butter
100g (3½oz) 70% dark chocolate,
  broken into pieces
300g (10½oz) marmalade

150g (5½oz) self-raising flour
pinch of salt
2 eggs, beaten

Makes 1 loaf

Preheat your oven to 180°C (350°F), Gas Mark 4, and line a 900-g (2-lb) loaf tin, or pour a little vegetable oil into the loaf tin and wipe it with a piece of kitchen paper so it is lightly oiled on all sides.

Melt the butter and chocolate over a low heat in a large saucepan. Don't be tempted to hurry it along with too much heat, as the butter will burn and the chocolate will split. When you have a lovely puddle of melted butter and chocolate in the pan, take it off the heat and stir in the marmalade.

Let it cool down a bit (there's enough time here to make a cup of tea) then pour the flour and salt into the pan and add the eggs on top. Stir it all around so it is well incorporated and then pour into the loaf tin. Bake for 30–35 minutes until cooked. Check by poking the cake with a skewer – it's ready when the skewer comes out clean. Leave to cool on a wire rack. This cake freezes well.

An Everyday Bara Brith

Bara brith is Welsh for 'speckled bread' – the speckles coming from the dried fruit that makes this a sort of cross between fruit cake and tea bread. It is comforting and filling and I love it, particularly because it saved me in an hour of need. I was four days into a nine-day walk, following the Wye Valley from mid-Wales to my home – a distance of 136 miles. I had covered about 70 long, steep, up and down miles by that point and thanks to rather damp weather, had had permanently wet feet. The result was spectacular blisters.

I had reached the hobbling, wincing stage and was still a good couple of miles from my campsite when I came upon a little café and art gallery in the village of Erwood. I'm not saying its bara brith was a miracle cure for blisters, but it cheered me up no end and gave me the strength to keep going until I could let blister plasters and Ibuprofen do their magic.

A quick note before you start – the fruit needs to be soaked overnight!

450g (1lb) mixed dried fruit

100g (3½oz) soft brown sugar

425ml (¾ pint) strong hot black tea
  (regular, Earl Grey or Lapsang
  Souchong)

450g (1lb) self-raising flour

1 teaspoon fine sea salt

1 teaspoon ground allspice

1 teaspoon mixed spice

1 large egg, beaten

Makes 1 loaf

Put the dried fruit and sugar into a bowl, pour over the hot tea and leave to soak overnight or for at least 5 hours.

When you are ready to cook, preheat your oven to 160°C (325°F), Gas Mark 3, and line a 900-g (2-lb) loaf tin. Stir the flour, salt and spices into your soaked fruit until everything is properly combined. Then add the beaten egg and mix again. You will end up with a lovely, fragrant, sticky, speckly dough!

Spoon the mixture into the lined tin and bake for 50–65 minutes, testing with a skewer. If it comes out clean your bara brith is ready. If you find it is getting too brown on the top, but is still not quite cooked, cover loosely with foil for the last bit of cooking. When it's done, take it out of the oven and let it cool in its tin for 20 minutes or so, then take it out and put it on a wire rack to cool completely. Cut into generous slices and spread as liberally as you like with butter. It freezes well.

A Festive Bara Brith

This is another Wright's Food Emporium special. Maryann made this wonderful adaptation as a bit of an experiment over Christmas. It sold like, well, hot cakes – and she was so inundated with orders for her festive bara brith

she could barely keep up. She shared her recipe with me, on condition that I help her with the orders next Christmas! Again, the fruit is soaked overnight so plan ahead.

120g (4½oz) dried cranberries

120g (4½oz) sultanas

2 tablespoons Welsh honey

a glug of Penderyn whisky (or any whisky)

160ml (5½fl oz) strong hot black tea, made using 2 teabags

225g (8oz) self-raising flour

50g (1¾oz) soft brown sugar

50ml (2fl oz) milk

1 large egg

zest and juice of 2 unwaxed clementines

Makes 1 loaf

Put the cranberries and sultanas in a bowl with the honey and whisky. Pour over the hot tea and leave to soak overnight.

When you are ready to cook, preheat your oven to 160°C (325°F), Gas Mark 3, and line a 900-g (2-lb) loaf tin. Add the flour and sugar to the dried fruit and mix well.

Then mix together the milk and egg and add, along with the clementine juice and zest. Mix again until everything is combined, pour into the tin and bake for about an hour, until your skewer comes out clean.

As before, cool in the tin and then on a wire rack. Maryann recommends this is eaten either with good Welsh butter or a slice of hard Welsh cheese, like Caws Cenarth or Hafod Cheddar.

SOME WINTER PICK-ME-UPS

~

Because every now and then, we have the kind of day that demands a pick-me-up.

How the Norwegians Stay Warm

The coldest temperatures I have ever endured were while filming in Siberia one December. It was regularly −40°C (−40°F), which freezes your eyelashes, hair, nose hairs (even if you don't think you have any) and makes breathing feel laboured – although that might have been partly due to the balaclava. But on a couple of occasions the temperature plummeted to below −50°C (−58°F), which is indescribable.

It was then that my friend and colleague, Alexis, who has filmed in some of the most extreme environments on earth, revealed this secret weapon to banish the chill. He had been given it while working in the Arctic with a team of Norwegian scientists. Perfectly qualified, then, to come up with a surefire way of beating the cold very pleasantly, even if just temporarily.

1 shot of whisky   1 shot of maple syrup

Serves 1

Pour the whisky into a mug and add the shot of maple syrup. Swirl around a bit and then down in one. Don't hang about. It might freeze.

Hot Lemon & Manuka Honey

I think quite a lot of us have our 'home cures', and this is mine. I honestly believe this simple concoction gets me through every winter. I will have it most mornings before I head out to feed the animals and any time I have that slightly achy or snivelly pre-cold feeling. Whether it is the combination of vitamin C in the lemon and the well-documented properties of Manuka honey, or whether it is entirely psychological, I don't know, but it seems to keep winter lurgies at bay.

juice of ½–1 lemon   1 generous teaspoon Manuka honey
boiling water

Serves 1

Use as much lemon juice as you like, depending on the juiciness of the lemon and how lemony you like things. Put the lemon juice in a large mug (something you can wrap your hands around, which also makes you feel better). Top up with boiling water and stir in the Manuka honey.

Hot Toddy   And to turn it into a hot toddy…add a shot of whisky or dark rum or brandy and a cinnamon stick.

Bullshot
with Chilli Sherry

A Thermos or hip flask of this on a winter walk warms even the coldest of toes. Don't even think about making your own consommé. It is a huge faff and takes ages. There is absolutely no shame in using the canned stuff. If you haven't made your Chilli Sherry yet, this will work with plain sherry, and will still be good, but you might want to make some for next time.

400ml (14oz) can beef consommé Tabasco
Chilli Sherry (see page 149) lemon juice
vodka salt and pepper
Worcestershire sauce

Serves 2–4

Heat the consommé until piping hot but not quite boiling.

Remove from the heat and add chilli sherry and vodka to taste. Spice up and season with Worcestershire sauce, Tabasco, salt, pepper and a squeeze of lemon. Yum.

+∿+

And that's it. Once you are replete, wrap up, snuggle down and spring will be here before we know it.

RESOURCES

Black Mountains Smokery – www.smoked-foods.co.uk

Chocolarder – www.chocolarder.com

Dough & Daughters – www.doughanddaughters.com

Esse – www.esse.com

Forage (Liz Knight) – www.foragefinefoods.com

Kingstone Brewery – www.kingstonebrewery.co.uk

Parva Spices – www.parva-spices.co.uk

Silver Circle Distillery – www.silvercircledistillery.com

Talgarth Mill – www.talgarthmill.com

The Preservation Society – www.thepreservationsociety.co.uk

Wright's Food Emporium – www.wrightsfood.co.uk

Wye Valley Meadery – www.wyevalleymeadery.co.uk

INDEX

AUTHOR'S ACKNOWLEDGEMENTS

It was Ben Frow and Emma Westcott of Channel 5 who came up with the idea of me cooking on telly – something I never imagined doing. So it is thanks to them, the team at Raise the Roof Productions and the viewers of *Escape to the Farm*, who sent me photos of my food they'd cooked and encouragement to write down the recipes, that I even considered doing this book.

As ever, support and invaluable advice from Stephanie Jackson and her team at Gaia – Alex Stetter, Caroline Brown and Megan Brown – and Rosemary Scoular at United Agents galvanized me into actually doing it. Thank you all.

And huge thanks and credit go to the people who inspired me and shared their recipes – my mum, Penny Johnstone, the team at Esse, Freddie Morland and family, Angharad Underwood, Ben at Parva Spices, Tim Maddams, Kate Colquhoun, Pooch Horsburgh and Maryann Wright.

Jonathan Atkinson deserves a special mention – and a lot of gin – for helping with an IT meltdown.

The book looks as beautiful as it does thanks to the design of Jonathan Christie, the patience and artistry of long-suffering photographer Andrew Montgomery, the generosity of Clare Bosanquet and the culinary skills of Pooch Horsburgh and Simone Shagam, who made my food look far better than I ever can!

Kate Strutt at Cabbages and Roses and Barbar at the Carrier Company – thank you both for giving me a sartorial elegance usually far beyond my reach.

And last, but perhaps most importantly of all, Tim and Sarah Stephens, my farming mentors and treasured friends, thank you for continuing to put up with all my nonsense!

Kate x

First published in Great Britain in 2022 by Gaia,
an imprint of
Octopus Publishing Group Ltd
Carmelite House, 50 Victoria Embankment, London EC4Y 0DZ
www.octopusbooks.co.uk

An Hachette UK Company
www.hachette.co.uk

ISBN 978-1-85675-462-0

A CIP catalogue record for this book is available from the British Library.
Printed and bound in Great Britain
10 9 8 7 6 5 4 3 2 1

Publisher: Stephanie Jackson
Creative Director: Jonathan Christie
Senior Editor: Alex Stetter
Photography: Andrew Montgomery
Home Economist: Anna Horsburgh
Assistant Home Economist: Simone Shagam
Senior Production Manager: Peter Hunt

Kate Humble is a writer, smallholder, campaigner and one of the UK's best-known TV presenters. She started her television career as a researcher, later presenting programmes such as 'Animal Park', 'Springwatch' and 'Autumnwatch', 'Lambing Live', 'Living with Nomads', 'Extreme Wives', 'Back to the Land', 'A Country Life for Half the Price' and 'Escape to the Farm'. Her book *Thinking on My Feet* was shortlisted for both the Wainwright Prize and the Edward Stanford Travel Memoir of the Year.

www.katehumble.com |  @katehumble | kmhumble

Also available: